Scar Light:
The Post-Trauma Glow of God's Presence

Kevin Hrebik, D.Min.

Foreword by Kaye Trickett

Other books by Kevin Hrebik:

- *Applying Faith and Family Systems to Emotional Scars: A 10-Week Curriculum*
- *Repurposing Scars: Meaningful Life after the Enduring Damage of Trauma*
- *The Special Message of Jesus' Scars*
- *The Carpenter's Shop and Other Metaphors*

DEDICATION

To scar bearers, broken folks, damaged souls, hollow
people, hopeless, downtrodden, oppressed, captives,
crushed, brokenhearted, decimated, shattered, and
anyone who has been hurt or suffered.

May you find the comfort, freedom, healing, peace,
release, joy, relief, hope, and soul light that only
Jesus, the Light of the World, can give you.

—Derived from Matt. 4:18

"Words which do not give
the light of Christ
increase the darkness."

Mother Teresa

CONTENTS

"When we consider that Christ is the true light,
having nothing in common with deceit,
we learn that our own life also must shine
with the rays of that true light."

Gregory of Nyssa (335–394 AD)

FOREWORD

I'm reminded of an old childhood song, but with an added twist, "Twinkle, twinkle little scar, tell the world how hurt you are" … but that's not the end of the story.

The book you hold in your hands is a Masterpiece. It is an invitation from the author, to know his Author—the only One who can piece us back together from what the world calls gory and use us for His Kingdom's glory.

Dr. Kevin Hrebik, aka forever "Chaplain Hrebik" to me, must hold a masters in mending (amongst the ranks of so many other letters that follow his name). His brilliant mind, once broken, has become the spoken and written wisdom of God for healing the broken who surround us.

I had the awesome opportunity to have served under his leadership his entire tenure as Chaplain at Plane State Jail, where he so tenderly tended his flock there. His was the voice of a gentle shepherd, healing, restoring, and leading the ladies. With a caring heart, he discipled them as Jesus would with truth and grace.

As you read this manuscript, may each word and footnote become a footprint as you follow Jesus, the Bright Morning Star Himself, into hope and healing, so you can go glowing to a dark, crooked, and depraved generation in which you shine like stars in the universe.

"I, Jesus, have sent my angel to testify to you of these things for the churches. I am the root and the descendent of David, the bright morning star" (Rev. 22:16).

When Jesus illuminates our lives, He transforms our scars into stars, rewriting our childhood song, "Twinkle, twinkle little star, glow and tell how healed you are!"

"So that you may become blameless and pure, 'children of God without fault in a warped and crooked generation.' Then you will shine among them like stars in the sky" (Phil. 2:15, NIV).

—Kaye Trickett, Founding Director,
C.H.A.R.M. Prison Ministry[1]

---

[1] Christ's Hope and Reconciliation Ministry (C.H.A.R.M.), https://charmprisonministry.org. See also p.19.

PREFACE

I recently came across the following poem from a woman named Whit (no last name given) from "Revive Your Roar," and it struck me that the words "scar light" could well be the phrase of the century:

> life looks good on you.
> but only after it kills you first.
>
> rockbottom blesses you
> with a different kind of beauty.
> the shine is survival.
>
> the glow is **scar-light.**
> every flicker you carry
> was forged in the dark.
>
> what they call light
> is the ash still burning.[2]

For years, I've been writing, teaching, and speaking about how God uses damaged people throughout scripture—from unlikely deliverers in the book of Judges (a left-handed man, a doubter, a woman, a luster, the son of a prostitute, and more!) and elsewhere in the Old Testament like David, the self-described sinner-in-chief, to the most unlikely authors of the New Testament (fishermen, tax collector, prosecutor of Christians, and

---

[2] Whit, *Revive Your Roar*,
https://www.facebook.com/photo.php?fbid=725006913902362&set=pb.
100091791788573.-2207520000&type=3, emphasis added.

more!). The point is how even the misfits and rejects among us, the scarred, damaged, broken, those with criminal records, former addicts, and those with the most unlikely of histories can become powerful witnesses and share our hard-won testimonies when we let God use us for His purposes, putting our broken pieces and parts into service for him.

This concept was the heart of my book *Repurposing Scars: Meaningful Life after the Enduring Damage of Trauma*, which came directly out of my doctoral project. From that, I hammered out a curriculum for inmates that I tested for more than three years with men at Harris County Jail, the third largest jail in the U.S., and then for ten years with women at the largest female prison in Texas. After so many years immersed in the material, I added the concept of "shame" to the original 8-concept theory, which was a no brainer to me since it was not only a concept by definition (universal to all people) but a major behavior driver. Many had written about Bowen's unfinished "9th concept," The Supernatural, and I added it as another concept (universal to all people), contributing my uniquely focused context to the work of many others like my friend, Dr. Robert Creech.[3]

During this time, I wrote *The Special Message of Jesus' Scars* as a gift book for the special people in our lives, especially our precious spiritual leaders and caregivers. The focus was on the fact that Jesus carried visible, tangible scars as He walked out of the tomb. I addressed it in a context other than the almost clichéd reference in the doubting Thomas narrative, which as I clearly point

---

[3] R. Robert Creech, *Family Systems in Congregation Life* (Grand Rapids: Baker Academic, 2019).

out, inadvertently occluded the real reason for Jesus' scars. My view went far beyond the Thomas narrative, and for me it's a tragedy that the real story has been overlooked by commentators and scholars ever since the first century. The pastor who wrote that book's Foreword said he had pastored for 40 years and never thought of Jesus' scars in that way before, but now he would never be able to think of them any other way.

I continued to refine my chosen subject material until it became a polished curriculum for inmates, who frequently said it was the best class they took during their entire time of incarceration. The title is, "Applying Faith and Family Systems to Emotional Scars," videos of which now have been uploaded to the Pando App for inmate tablets nationwide and YouTube, ideally for their families to study, learn, and grow along with them. Search for these videos on YouTube using "When Jesus Meets Your Scars."[4]

The reason this material has been so effective among arguably the most damaged population anywhere is because of the principle of God's "transformative intervention"[5]—first experienced at salvation, and then as stages and milestones of growth throughout our Christian life are cumulatively added to our ever-expanding testimony. God doesn't just save us; His very touch transforms; His presence alone creates irreversible

---

[4] Kevin Hrebik, "When Jesus Meets Your Scars," 12 Lessons, https://www.youtube.com/results?search_query=when+jesus+meets+your+scars.

[5] Walter Brueggemann, *The Message of the Psalms* (Minneapolis: Augsburg, 1984), 162.

changes within every part of our beings; His light continually drives out the darkness within us.

In 2025, I taught a series of classes at my church titled, "When Jesus Meets Your Scars, Everything Changes." This was a spinoff of a series following my pastor's recent sermon series by a similar title. Nothing is the same after Jesus' touch, and the afterglow of His presence in the wake of trauma is a particularly beautiful way to put that illuminated transformation into words.

Welcome to this latest effort in my lifetime work and calling to minister via writing, teaching, and video to the broken and broken-hearted among us—the least of these, in Jesus' words: "And the King will answer and say to them, 'Truly I say to you, to the extent that you did it for one of the least of these brothers or sisters of mine, you did it for me'" (Matt. 25:40).[6]

Designed as a gift book, you might think about the special, caring souls in your life, those who first brought the light to you, those who continue to minister light to you, and those who are your companions and fellow light bearers. Like you, they are called to go to people who have known great darkness, to the above damaged souls who now light their corner of the world with their own hard-won "scar light." Of course, let me be clear that ALL light bearers are included in the "Gospel light spectrum" and would appreciate your caring gesture.

—Kevin Hrebik

---

[6] Unless otherwise noted, all quoted verses are from the New American Standard (NASB) version. Using BlueLetterBible.org as my primary lexicon, the choice is NASB20.

1. Scar Light:
Forged in Darkness

Like the poem in the Preface intimates, the more damage that people have incurred, and the harder they hit rock bottom, the bigger the glow they carry out of that forging, formative furnace. Some not only have been to rock bottom, but they have camped out there, and like me, they even tried digging holes in the bottom of rock bottom. The death at rock bottom is real in every sense, except your heart is still beating. Survivors have experienced soul death, spirit death, social death, mind and heart death, and every other form of dying except the final release from life. But many of us tried that, too, sometimes more than once.

The late, great modern apologist, intellectual, and profound thinker and writer of our modern era, C. S. Lewis, wrote a book called *Surprised by Joy*, which was his testimony of coming to salvation through his wife, whose name was Joy. He later wrote in another book that "Joy is the serious business of heaven."[7] This is the different kind of beauty that is proof positive of having been rescued from rock bottom, the surviving "beauty" and "shine" of which is Jesus' sublime but undeniable presence. Survivors often call this coming out of the fire without smelling like smoke.

Whit calling that after-trauma glow "scar light" inspired me to my core—it was literally the perfect word art to paint the picture of what happens to deeply damaged people when the light of the world touches and transforms them and all their shattered pieces. These deeply redeemed souls then have something powerful to say to the suffering world around them. What may seem like only a flicker at our first glance as newborn babes, we learn soon enough in reality is His formidable presence within, which goes before us into battle against all the many forms of darkness (Deut. 20:4; Zech. 4:6).

This is a strength beyond the power of human intellect to grasp, because it's often revealed in surprising ways, like humble joy (Neh. 8:10). But the bearers of that joy remember the searing fires of rock bottom that once threatened to devour them. For them, the punishing heat was transformed into a purging, purifying flame, around which they would wrap their hearts and souls. It became a fierce kind of burning strength that could withstand all the forces of evil and emerge the winner.

The raw strength of such joy comes straight from heaven's purest, white-hot light, a dazzling foretaste of eternity. It's the surviving, glowing embers of the forging

---

[7] C. S. Lewis, *Letters to Malcolm: Chiefly on Prayer* (San Diego: Harvest, 1964), 92-93.

fire that dared to defy the gravitational forces of rock bottom, that dared to stand tall among the smoldering devastation around them, that dared to embrace joy and smile (imagine!) after so much assault and every attempt to destroy them. Lewis referenced "that hideous strength" in one title of his science fiction trilogy.[8]

"Embracing the embers," as one friend described it, is the epitome of what's known as testimony, knowing that the trial has smelted soul steel, which has emerged looking like patience, kindness, goodness, faithfulness. This now shiny ball of survival looks like radiant peace, irrepressible joy, and the light of love. Because it's just too important to keep such a glowing treasure to ourselves, it almost demands to be spread to others, candle to candle, even to the least of these, even to the ends of the earth. The results are capable of transcending the world, one soul at a time, ascending from the ashes:

> From messes … to messages
> From tests … to testimonies
> From trials … to triumphs
> From blindness … to sight
> From negative … to positive
> From hurt … to healing
> From stubborn … to steadfast
> From empty … to overflowing
> From great darkness … to eternal light
> From sickness … to wholeness
> From broken pieces … to beautiful mosaics
> From scars … to scar light

---

[8] C. S. Lewis, *The Space Trilogy: Out of the Silent Planet, Perelandra, That Hideous Strength* (NY: Simon and Schuster, 2011).

Relating to the above is the following from *The Special Message of Jesus Scars*:

> [While] standing in your own "mess in process" …
> God steers you to someone else in the same place, at
> which time you learn a precious lesson about
> receiving and giving grace simultaneously. Remember
> the process for which Jesus personally paved the
> way—your moment of truth, soul-searching prayer,
> trusting God's judgment, dying to self, rising to new
> life, complete before and after testimony, then
> walking into your mission, calling, and purpose. This
> final stage of putting yourself and your mosaic of
> brokenness into His service comprises the full circle
> message of Jesus' scars.[9]

We speak the language of suffering fluently because it
was our daily sustenance; we suckled from it and then
cut our first baby teeth on it, and we are intimately
familiar with every dialect and idiom. Albeit unwillingly,
having become viscerally familiar with rock bottom
developed in us a keen eyesight in near pitch darkness.
We found we could maneuver around well, despite the
fact that we couldn't escape its clutches.

Something else that grew, imperceptibly at first, was a
new glow within—perhaps it was our night vision turned
inward—but despite the despair and devastation that
threatened to strangle us in its choke hold, we learned to
discern even the faintest of lights. The closer we came to
seeing our way out, the closer something within us knew
we were soon going to say, "your love broke through,"

---

[9] Kevin Hrebik, *The Special Message of Jesus' Scars* (Amazon: KDP,
2023), 66-7.

as classic guitarist Phil Keaggy worded it.[10] In this context, I would say, "until your light burned through."

Moreover, we became positive with each trembling step that we were seeing the early stages of a budding gift of artistic expression amidst the ruin. Thus blossomed a gift that could only be forged here, on the very basement floor of life, a place void of hope, peace, and joy, but it was a gift that was patiently and expertly crafted by all-seeing and all-knowing hands, one that we took with us when we finally experienced our first gasp of true freedom. Now we have something to say to others freshly released, and even those desperate to walk free but who remain impossibly tethered to that awful bottom. We know their stories inside out, and we have empathy for them no matter how chilling their witness.

We were first their friends in solidarity; we then became their reliable guides, all inspired by our own unforgettable time of having been "on our knees on the holy ground of sorrow."[11] We moved efficiently, like ghosts in the night, through the messes and tangles, the pitfalls and perils, knowing the way out, knowing whose hand we were reaching for on their behalf. We followed a mere inkling of light until it engulfed us wholesale.

We emerged with a glow lit by the very fire of heaven, something beyond earthly understanding because it is far beyond the grasp of mortal minds. We knew freedom like we knew our own pain; we knew it in

---

[10] Phil Keaggy, "Your Love Broke Through," Album and Song (New Song Records, 1979).

[11] Francis Weller, *The Wild Edge of Sorrow: Rituals of Renewal and the Sacred Work of Grief* (Berkeley, CA: North Atlantic Books, 2015).

our knower, a branded, soul knowing—it was an unutterable bond with pierced hands that also had suffered incalculably, but from whose grasp nothing in the universe could separate or tear asunder (Rom. 8:38).

Several other examples of such fire-tested souls are in Chapter 3, but I want to mention a particular couple, Charity and Jeff Fyke, who run a transitional housing ministry, Oaks of Righteousness, which now has four homes. Founded by Beth Whittier in 2012, doors opened in 2014, and while they have a total recidivism rate of 5.2%, they have had zero return to prison since 2018. One who now works at Oaks, Tosha Rose, was the only faith-based dorm mentor to hold that role 3 times during my tenure as Chaplain, and she is my first protégé to teach my family systems course to fellow residents. It's almost like a homecoming whenever I go to the ministry because I knew most of them when they were inmates, but once they were touched by God, their lives were never the same, as proven by their profound and beautifully fruitful transformations.

Perhaps one of the best parts of our new life is we found that we could, in a sense, paint with light, like our fingers were His paintbrushes! Within our previously empty brokenness we discovered wells of light ink, and we found we could paint all the colors of His light onto other broken hearts. We became light bearers, light carriers, and light artists—all because we met the Master Artist, and he first painted all over our brokenness with His healing light. The glow of His brushstrokes brought our scars to life in living color. "Remember those earlier days after you had received the light, when you endured in a great conflict of suffering" (Heb. 10:32, NIV).

2. God's Presence as Light

God's presence in the Old Testament truly would have been something mind-blowing. So many of His actions then were far more glorious and "over the top" than we experience today. Splitting the entire Red Sea so millions of released Hebrew slaves could walk across on dry ground? Then releasing the water to drown the pursuing Egyptian army? This is the stuff of movies and legends, like Charleston Heston's classic *The Ten Commandments*. Indeed, I daresay most can't even fathom our sovereign Lord performing something like that in our modern world.

Prior to the great separation of the sea, God's other miracles in the Exodus deliverance were equally extravagant and ostentatious. A total of ten plagues, any one of which would send today's population to "critical mass"—our soft generation reacting and overreacting like so many spoiled children, for whom "trauma" mostly comes in the form of ubiquitous "offenses" over everything, literally from A-Z. Even one actual plague, for instance COVID-19, sent the whole world into a giant tailspin and collective panic. Imagine nine others in rapid succession. People today would be in full blown anarchy, and other than hard-core believers, would be cursing God, His people, and everything related.

Once safely away from the impending Egyptians, the Israelites entered a protracted time of testing in the wilderness. Throughout their wandering, however, God guided them directly—a pillar of cloud by day and a pillar of fire by night (Exod. 13:20-22). The light became known as the "Shekinah glory," which is not a biblical word, but rather a Hebrew word derivative referencing God's presence. Following is a helpful description:

> The word *shekinah* does not appear in the Bible, but the concept clearly does. The Jewish rabbis coined this extra-biblical expression, a form of a Hebrew word that literally means "he caused to dwell," signifying that it was a divine visitation of the presence or dwelling of the Lord God on this earth.[12]

---

[12] From https://www.gotquestions.org/shekinah-glory.html.

It was in the wilderness that God gave instructions to Moses to build a portable Tabernacle. When I toured Israel in 2004, our group visited the full-scale model of that wilderness Tabernacle, shown above.[13] Outside are the scripturally ordered objects: the altar of burnt offering and the bronze basin. Inside as well are the required artifacts: the golden lampstand, the table of showbread, the altar of incense, and the ark of the covenant with two golden cherubim stretching their wings over the mercy seat (Exod. 25).[14]

Scripture tells us that when sacrifices pleased God in the Tabernacle, the place was filled with His glory (Exod. 40:34-38). All the manifestations of God as light in the Old Testament were patterns that Jesus fulfilled in the New Testament, when He said, to the shock and dismay of the Pharisees, "I am the light of the world" (John 8:12). The following comment is well phrased: "Just as the divine Presence dwelled in a relatively plain tent called the 'tabernacle' before the Temple in Jerusalem

---

[13] From www.holylandsite.com.
[14] From www.Biblelieux.com

was built, so did the Presence dwell in the relatively plain man who was Jesus."[15]

When King Solomon constructed the original, permanent Temple in Jerusalem, it contained the same artifacts brought there from the wilderness Tabernacle. The Temple was not just a place of worship but "a divine residence" as one writer put it. During the Temple's dedication, the glory of the Lord visibly filled the place, again signifying God's presence: "And when the priests came out of the Holy Place, the cloud filled the house of the Lord, so that the priests could not stand there to minister because of the cloud; for the glory of the Lord filled the house of the Lord" (1 Kings 8:10-11).

The theme of God's presence appearing as light continued into the New Testament, first in the person of Jesus, the Way, the Truth, and the Light of the world from its creation (John 1:1-51; John 8:12; John 9:5 et al.). Then, after Jesus' ascension, the Holy Spirit appeared as tongues of fire in Acts 2:1-3. This was yet another vital transition in the biblical history of God's presence with humankind. Now we ourselves had become God's dwelling place, His human house. 1 Cor. 3:16 says, "Do you not know that you yourselves are God's temple and that God's Spirit dwells in you?"

Too often, however, this holy and sacred continuity of God's presence has been reduced to the contentious subject of speaking in tongues, like that's the only reason Acts 2 is in scripture. Sometimes, this tragic sub-focus even overshadows our empowerment to speak God's

---

[15] From https://bible.knowing-jesus.com/topics/God~s-Shekinah-Glory.

truth to *draw others to Him,* and the lifetime role of the
Holy Spirit to *draw us closer to God.* For some, everything
else is subjugated to whether or not someone speaks in
tongues. I once saw a woman literally holding an
inmate's jaw and lightly slapping her face, "Just loosen
your tongue," she kept saying, like it was the most urgent
thing in the world. Others try to combine the "baptism
of the Holy Spirit" with water baptism—which
conflation waters down and detracts from both events.

The following speaks directly to the true intent and
original magnitude of the light of God's presence:

> Through the Holy Spirit, each of us [like the
> disciples] can also receive the ability to *speak God's
> truth,* empowering us to share our faith and inspire
> others around us. This powerful gift reminds us that
> we are never alone; God's presence ignites a spark
> within our hearts, urging us to fulfill His purpose.
> The experience encourages us to connect more
> deeply with the Holy Spirit, leading our lives in *love
> and service to others.*[16]

This brief biblical history of God's presence as light
leads directly to this book's context, which follows Jesus'
own witness post-resurrection, transferred to His hand-
selected witnesses, which in turn was transferred to those
witnesses ever since, including those who carry His light
despite their scars, emotional damage, and all the many
forms of trauma. In fact, the light the scarred carry is
unique and precious because of the depth of the damage
life brought their way; it's light of a different hue because

---

[16] From https://biblerepository.com/bible-verses-about-tongues-of-fire/, emphasis added.

of the special crucible in which it was forged. And then one glorious day, we will see Him face to face, fully beholding His glory, and unlike Moses (Exod. 3:6), we will be able to stand within the direct presence of His heavenly, blindingly radiant light.

Whenever people say they don't have a dramatic testimony to compare to all those with shocking "before" stories, I always tell them to be grateful they didn't get so far away from the light that when they saw it for the first time it was a shock to the system. Tongue-in-cheek, I tell them to make sure they don't go wild just to have a better testimony. Our darkness was a foil for His light; the level of our suffering only made spiritual sight that much more treasured. Healing is a gradual process that starts with His light touching our spiritually blind eyes, and then it begins to move through every part of us, leaving nothing untouched. As a man named Balt Rodriguez said, "It's strange how healing doesn't announce itself; one day you just notice the weight you carried wasn't so heavy anymore."[17]

Soon enough, as His light wells up within and overflows into love and service, we naturally desire to share our healing-in-process with others who are hurting like we were. So, the story of light continues from Creation to the Tabernacle, to the Temple, to Jesus, to the Holy Spirit, to us, and now we pass the torch of His light to others. The same eternal light leads us all toward our final, resplendent eternity!

---

[17] Balt Rodriguez, PTSD: The War Within, https://www.facebook.com/photo/?fbid=1264346839050479&set=a.56 1214229363747.

3. The Sweet Oil of Crushing

I recently heard it said that "ministry is others being blessed by the oil that crushed you." Included in my above-mentioned tour of Israel was the opportunity to see the tools the ancients used to extract oil from olives. I took the above pic in a recreated first-century village in Nazareth.[18] Clearly, it takes extreme pressure to extract oil from olives, which squares well with life experiences during "crushing times." It's hard to see in this photo, but there is a large groove in the rock where the oil ran down from the pressure of the press with its large, weighted lever.

---

[18] See https://nazarethvillage.com/about/.

Olive oil was used for many practical purposes in the early centuries of civilization, such as lamps, among other things, and it is mentioned prolifically in Scripture. It lit people's homes and places of worship and allowed them to travel and gather after dark. As one source aptly described it, "This basic need for light to push back the darkness naturally became a picture of God's spiritual light and His guidance in our lives."[19]

Oil was used in food, as a means of healing, such as Isaiah described (Isa. 1:6), and an element in grooming, like when Esther prepared herself to meet the King (Est. 2:12). It was an expression of hospitality (Luke 7:46) and part of the burial process, including the anointing of Jesus' body (Mark 16:1). Below is a profound summary:

> Because oil was so valuable and necessary in so many parts of their daily lives, it was the perfect thing for God to choose as a symbol for His most precious spiritual gifts—His presence, His blessing, His very life![20]

Oil has many sacred uses in scripture, such as anointing the Tabernacle and its furnishings (Exod. 30:26-29); also, holy anointing oil, for which God himself prescribed the recipe (vv. 23-25), which was forbidden for personal use: "It is holy, and it shall be holy to you." One commentator worded it like this: "It became *His* special oil for *His* special purposes, turning

---

[19] Christian Pure Staff, "Bible Study: Oil in Scripture and its Hidden Layers of Meaning," https://christianpure.com/learn/oil-in-scripture-meaning/.
[20] Ibid.

ordinary things into something extraordinarily sacred because *He* said so!"[21]

Other sacred uses of oil were for anointing Priests like Aaron (Exod. 29:7), Kings like David (1 Sam. 16:13), and Prophets like Elisha (1 Kings 19:16). It was used as part of sacrificial offerings (Lev. 2), and it was part of Jacob's ritual naming of Bethel as the place of his ladder to heaven dream, which meant "house of God" (Gen. 28:18). Indeed, the process of making things holy and set apart for holy purposes "lays the groundwork for the New Testament, where we learn that believers are 'set apart' by the Holy Spirit, who is so often pictured by oil."[22]

Scripture describes oil as the quintessential symbol and metaphor of God's presence and power—as empowerment for divine service (1 Sam. 16:13), healing and spiritual restoration (Ezek. 16:9), illumination and divine guidance, preservation, blessing, and joy (Psalm 45:7; Heb. 1:9), and flowing, permeating influence (Psalm 133).

Think about the basic process of extracting the oil, which is the same even with modern electronic presses. The olives are put in a device where they can be crushed—not unlike how God steers us into trials that are meant to purge us of our sins and make us holy (Mal. 3:3). There is a device capable of doing the crushing— not unlike how our sovereign God carefully orchestrates painful, stressful events and circumstances in our lives to stretch, test, and mature us (1 Pet. 1:7). In the end, the

---

[21] "Bible Study: Oil in Scripture and its Hidden Layers of Meaning."
[22] Ibid.

trials or tests produce the precious oil, which wouldn't exist without the crushing process, but now is a precious product with an abundance of usefulness—not the least of which is to be a source of God's glory: "For our light and momentary troubles are achieving for us an eternal glory that far outweighs them all" (2 Cor. 4:17). Not a lot different than trimming oil lamps until the flame burns clean, so we are prepared through trimming for ministry and leadership until we burn with pure flames.

This non-exhaustive summary helps reinforce the biblical background undergirding this book, and by direct extension the numerous examples of ministry by the crushed to the crushed. One of the first things I noticed as a prison chaplain was just how many prison ministries there were (I oversaw 50+ at just one unit). I met many former inmates now anointed and called to minister to others who wore the white uniforms they once wore. I saw former addicts and hardened criminals with multiple felonies, now transformed and called to a higher purpose than being a rebel and serving self or the enemy. Instead, they now maintain a renunciation of the enemy of human souls, while making an ongoing sacrifice of self in the service of God and others.

Something I have communicated hundreds of times is that the moment we take our eyes off ourselves and put them on others (I use the classic finger pointed to me, then turn it to point outward), that's when we start to mature. When it's suddenly no longer all about us, like so many perennial teenagers no matter their age, that's when God can start to use us in His service, because the Christian life always has been and always will be about loving and serving others. Regardless of how many bad witnesses over the centuries have brought shame to the body of witnesses called the church, the simple truth is that God still speaks the same truth to every person, and that never has, nor will it ever change. What we do with His truth and His sacred duty is the only variable.

I want to mention a few of these transformed servants by name. John Downs was Senior Staff Chaplain at Harris County Jail in Houston for many years. Formerly convicted of 8 felonies, he now is one of the sweetest, most selfless men I've ever met—and he made amends to many of the victims of his crimes, often to their great surprise. He is the picture of inspiration, humble to a fault, and he has a delightful sense of humor. He would do anything for anyone, and God used him in a powerful way in my life.

John is the one who got me involved with prison ministry. He is the kind of person who leads by example, and I wanted to be like him. The story of our meeting was humorously captured in a recent podcast interview when I was asked how I got started in this line of work.[23] I told them that we had a seminary assignment to visit a ministry we'd never been to before, spend 4 hours, and write a paper. The laugh was when Daniel observed that I could have gone anywhere, but I chose jail of all places. Josh chimed in saying, "You could have picked Chick-Fil-A, and this would be a whole different interview." What started so simply, writing a seminary paper, resulted in God's enduring call on my life.

---

[23] Daniel Salcy, Josh Duffy, and Kevin Hrebik, "A Prison Story," 1LoveHTX Podcast (Season 4, Episode 112, 14:20), https://www.youtube.com/watch?v=t6TghB2f9gw.

The reason prison ministry worked for me was because I related to and empathized with the inmates' stories, because in many ways they were all echoes and variations of my own chaos turned into service. I didn't need years of experience before strongly sensing God's call on my life, which remains intact to the present, albeit in a different form in retirement. We may retire from a career, but we don't retire from our calling. Trauma recognizes trauma in others; it's a type of instant "life cred" among those who know and recognize it. I've always said that I can tell by looking someone in the eye whether they have suffered greatly in life.

The following testimony from Naomi Reed, a longtime prison ministry volunteer, is one of the most cringeworthy I have heard, and I have heard many grisly stories, but today she is one of the most sincere, kindest, and most empathetic people you could meet.

"The home I grew up in was one where domestic violence was an everyday occurrence. This affected the things I would accept in my life as an adult. As I found myself in abusive relationships, I would always overlook the violence they would inflict on me. I always had a black eye or a busted lip. Emotional and verbal abuse always just came with the territory. The emotional pain seemed to be too much at times, but just when l thought things could not get any worse, they always did.

"My ex-husband, a former Sergeant in the Marines, would lock me in a closet and pace back and forth telling me to get ready to die while aiming his loaded gun at me. Once after an argument, he ran over me with his car, leaving me disfigured for life. Turning to drugs and

18

alcohol as my coping escape then landed me in prison wondering how my life turned out this way.

"Throughout all the years of this brokenness of my soul, I always had a little glimpse of hope that maybe, just maybe, my life someday would be full of love, peace, and joy. I would say 'hope the size of a mustard seed.' One day in 2002, I was invited to church where I heard a message about a man named Jesus, that he was the Son of God who died on the cross, and if I believed in him, I would be forgiven of my sins and given a brand-new life. I said a prayer that day and I was surely given a new life. I was set free from believing I was unworthy of being loved and being treated as a child of God.

"Today, I have been healed of my past wounds, and I am happily married to a man of God who treats me like a princess and only speaks words that build me up rather than tear me down. God has turned my ashes into beauty and has taken what the devil meant for evil and used it for his glory. I am so honored to go back into the very same prison where I served time, and now get to share my experience, strength, and hope with women who have lost hope."

The Foreword writer, Kaye, and her husband David Trickett, are both former inmates who now run a large, thriving prison ministry that maintains a strong presence in multiple units. For more than 25 years, they have conducted church services, Bible studies, mentoring, discipleship, and prayer. They have hosted numerous special events like Day with Dad, Day with Mom, basketball tournaments, feeding staff, and more, plus they run 7 transitional houses.

Eugenia Valencia, who I met through Kaye's ministry at the unit where I served, has perhaps the most bone-chilling story of all. She recently published her autobiography, *Perfectly ~~Un~~loved: A True Story of Triumph over Darkness*, and the following is from a description I wrote during the process of helping her edit her book:

"Inspired by true events, *Perfectly ~~Un~~Loved* is a heart-wrenching but hope-filled journey of trauma, survival, divine encounters, and the miraculous power of God.

"Abandoned at birth to die on a windowsill in a Russian prison, Eugenia's life began in the shadow of death. Miraculously rescued by a prison nurse, she was placed into the state-run orphanage system, where she endured a brutal, traumatic childhood of abuse, hunger, neglect, and violence.

"Amid the chaos and brutality, she becomes a fierce but respected 'gang leader' among her fellow orphans-until a young girl named Julia arrived, carrying things that were foreign to her: a Bible, an unshakable light, and the Gospel of Salvation. Suddenly, her world was turned upside down, and she was torn between survival and surrender, between rage and redemption.

"Eugenia's story will shock you and leave you in awe with inspiration proving that hope can grow in the darkest and most destitute places."

As I got to know Eugenia, I began to learn just how much our histories overlapped. We began to swap "shock" stories, and I realized I had found a rare kindred spirit. As stated elsewhere, those who have suffered extensively in life speak a unique language, and whose surviving scars are only understood by those fluent with that particular jargon. After finding salvation in the dark world of the orphanage, she became driven to find purpose after her years of chaos. Pushing herself hard to learn English, she then earned two master's degrees, left her native country, married a godly man who is a NASA flight surgeon, and she now is a mother of two beautiful children. At the time of writing, she was working for the state of Texas in the field of human trafficking.

Through the many months of laboring over her manuscript with her, I learned some valuable lessons. Whether acquired during a dance with death for her first six months of life as an extreme preemie, followed by an extreme childhood across three poverty-level orphanages in Russia—or a sadistic, alcoholic, enraged father in rural Wisconsin, feeding his multiple vices instead of feeding and clothing his family, then using his booze soaked, neurotic brain to creatively torture all of them—pain is pain, and scars are scars. However similar or dissimilar our B.C. stories (before Christ), we also shared the bright, saving, delivering, and healing light of Christ's loving presence. Ours were only two stories among so many others, many of which I mention here, that truly were transformed into triumphs over darkness.

Brad Gardner is a former drug addict, drug dealer, and criminal who after conversion in 1978 has spent the last 43 years volunteering in TDCJ. In that time, he has ministered on 33 different units including Death Row in the Polunsky Unit for 4 years. In those decades, he has worked under 110 different Chaplains. He became the director of Prisoners Bible Institute in 2015, a prison revival ministry that has spanned almost five decades, and by God's grace continues to bring the Gospel of Christ into TDCJ on a weekly basis. He also donates hygiene supplies, Bibles, and other items as needed to multiple different units.

Bill Everts, one of my best friends, fellow servant, and Executive Director of Less than the Least Ministries, has served a good bit of time but now is at the helm of one of the best prison ministries around, ministering in multiple units, conducting services, discipleship classes, managing podcasts, and always giving to support needs like Bibles, hygiene supplies, and more. He and his wife, Stephanie, are both musicians and they truly make beautiful music together. Adding his mad studio and creative skills, together they blazed a trail on the now nationwide Pando App for inmate tablets—the single best paradigm shift in incarceration in our modern era. Bill is another one with a painful past but who today is known for his huge heart and great sense of humor.

A man named Jesus Lopez had a 147-year sentence as a major drug dealer, but upon gaining parole now runs a prison ministry called Last Call. His most memorable words for me were, "Once I smuggled drugs out of Mexico; now I smuggle hygiene and fried chicken back in." Once, he was car-jacked a mile from the border reentering the U.S., and they took not only all his sound equipment but his van as well—they had to walk the rest of the way. Not to be deterred from his calling, he replaced what was stolen and continued to minister to inmates. I always looked forward to his ministry coming to the unit, and he literally is the sweetest, humblest man you'll ever meet.

The examples are too numerous to name, but the point is the same—it was because God transformed, healed, inspired, anointed, and set them apart for His work that they took up their crosses, took their eyes off of themselves, put their damage into His service. They began reaching souls far and wide with God's light, love, and truth. They went to the "the least of these," whom many ignore, the outcasts and modern lepers like they once were themselves. This is living scar light in action; this is shining a light in the darkness, especially the unique, soul-consuming darkness of prisons.

The above, and so many more like us, now succeed because we speak the language of pain, have crash landed on rock bottom, have experienced the fiery purging of the pit, and have learned intimately the strength of the forces seeking to steal, kill, and destroy our mind, body, and spirit (John 10:10). It was then, in that merciless furnace, that we found His greater strength arising within us to overcome even soul death. The best was when we found true freedom by His healing hand that cured our blindness like the man born blind in John 9 (who is all of us). We rose from the mats that held our broken bodies captive (John 5); we ascended from our premature cremation ashes, like a great army of former misfits and rejects now transformed into so many unlikely, soaring Phoenixes.

The sweet oil of crushing is ignited by God's own flames of passion and service, lighting our hearts and then the world around us, one corner at a time, one hurting soul at a time. First, everything changes within when we were crushed with divine purpose to produce the precious oil of anointed service. Then we made a miraculous flight out of our desert deaths, born again to a new life, and we flew straight into the warm embrace of His freedom, glowing brightly with His joy, ready, willing, and able to light others' pathways and guide them directly to the Father of Lights (James 1:17).

There is no shame in being crushed, broken, and shattered; in fact, there is no oil without it, and without oil there is no light. Funny how that works, how our breaking process releases the power of His Light process. But then we became unique, living light stories, raised to life after our own tango with death, just like Jesus' own Friday and Sunday—which in turn became our own Friday and Sunday, sacred before and after stories, mirroring His ultimate with our just enough, just as I am … but then through us, others see the Light, hear the Truth, and then find the Way.

As if inspired by the cover image, one poet described light as something that can be poured. My pastor frequently refers to how we must lean toward God if we want Him to pour into us. Yet, we can't pour anything if our well is empty—we can't pour light, love, grace, joy, or forgiveness. When we are first filled, however, everything changes. Now we pour freely because that is the nature of every good gift from the Father—we pour out of our abundance, and He keeps on filling us.

It's been aptly stated that you can't outgive God, but it applies to much more than money. We become like the widow ministering to Elijah, "The bowl of flour was not used up, nor did the jar of oil become empty, in accordance with the word of the Lord, which He spoke through Elijah" (1 Kings 17:16).

4. Our Inner Light Is Portable

"People are like stained glass windows. They sparkle and shine when the sun is out, but when the darkness sets in, their beauty is revealed only if there is a light from within."[24] I'm probably going to use this quote in every book I write, not just because it's so uncannily accurate, but because the author is an expert on grief, a state of heart into which I was born, have lived in long-term, and the subject on which I cut my teeth as a budding chaplain.

So many famous sayings on inner light through the ages come to mind, with these few being among the many hundreds I could have quoted: "The eyes are the

---

[24] Elizabeth Kübler-Ross, as quoted in Jim Clemmer, *The Leader's Digest: Timeless Principles for Team and Organization* (Kitchner, Ontario: Clemmer Group, 2003), 84.

window to the soul," "A heart full of kindness glows different," "Beauty is not in the face; beauty is a light in the heart." The more we learn and live the principle, the more we become who we are representing: "As we open our hearts to others, we begin to discover the truth of our own inner beauty, inner strength, and inner light."[25] Perhaps the most famous words on the subject are by universally esteemed civil rights leader and martyr, Dr. Martin Luther King, Jr., "Darkness cannot drive out darkness; only light can do that. Hate cannot drive out hate; only love can do that."

Scripture affirms, "For at one time you were darkness, but now you are light in the world. Walk as children of light" (Eph. 5:8). At the same time, scripture also warns, "The eye is the lamp of the body. So, if your eye is healthy, your whole body will be full of light, but if your eye is bad, your whole body will be full of darkness. If then the light in you is darkness, how great is the darkness!" (Matt. 6:22-23).

As I've often said, every trauma is some kind of loss, and the most severe among them comprise the greatest sources of grief—loss of innocence, loss of a childhood, loss of one's sense of safety, trust, and hope in the world. Especially when these traumas happen to the young, and when they are egregious, they cause tragic soul disfigurement before the child can develop strength to resist, much less manage or even comprehend. This invasive, inner damage—emotional, physical, and mental scarring—has been at the center of my life work and calling. It's one thing to learn to accept the reality of, and

---

[25] A-Z Quotes, "Inner Light," https://www.azquotes.com/quotes/topics/inner-light.html

even to find new meaning for the loss of a precious loved one. It's quite another to learn to accept that your childhood was decimated and then to realize the whole of it was an irretrievable loss. It's quite another thing to realize that everything that should have been important to a child was not only taken away but replaced with something destructive.

To move into Kübler-Ross's famous fifth stage of grief—acceptance—of that kind of cruel Goliath, is a challenge with which thankfully the minority of humans have had to grapple. To move beyond acceptance into the relatively new field of the sixth stage—meaning making—is to move into the work of another favorite author on the subject, Melissa Kelly. Hear her words of wisdom, which further illustrate the stained-glass image, and are particularly poignant in the context of both early life and unjust trauma such as criminal abuse:

> Mosaics emerge from brokenness. They are made of pieces, fragments, and shards; they are marked by spaces, gaps, and cracks. The mosaic of grief also emerges from brokenness. After loss, our lives may feel shattered and in pieces, and we may feel we are alone with our brokenness and suffering. But we are not alone. God's love, the heart of reality, holds us in the brokenness of grief.[26]

Learning to unlearn is the universal work of scar bearers, especially those who also are learning to wield powerful scripture swords, sharpened by truth and penetrating our innermost parts with light (2 Tim. 2:15).

---

[26] Melissa Kelley, *Grief: Contemporary Theory and the Practice of Ministry* (Minneapolis: Fortress Press, 2010), 117.

We don't all start on a level playing field—some have a greater handicap at the starting line, they bring fewer strengths that others take for granted; instead, they bring only steely grit and a hard-boiled focus that were daily survival skills. We don't take trust for granted, nor do we even assume it exists. We don't have naturally sunny beliefs; we have to labor to overcome the many powerful negatives. When we finally learn the power of positives, however, we then become unstoppable. When we finally learn the power of prayer to overcome deeply gnawing doubts, fears, insecurities, and even simple worries, we then become confident to a flaw and then begin toppling ever greater obstacles … and yes, Goliaths, too.

A part of trauma recovery with which I keenly empathize is the matter of becoming a witness, and how difficult and intimidating that can be for some. Many find that they have a lot to say but don't always have the ability to put what's in their heart into words. They share what I call the newly released POW (prisoner of war) deer in the headlights look. So, they become a type of "undercover" Christian, as some harshly describe them. They aren't overt about their hard-won faith and deliverance, but their message is no less genuine.

The truth is that anyone can learn the spiritual side of life; anyone can find salvation—the one and only requirement is *humility*, in which every scarred person has been thoroughly sautéed. While literally anyone in the world can find God's peace, light, joy, and presence, you can't teach trauma strength; you can't instruct someone on how light exudes from scars; you simply can't learn such things other than in life's hottest ovens. So, whether they lack eloquence or a dynamic speaking presence, they have done the heaviest lifting of all, as they have made a most miraculous exodus from arguably the hardest Egypt of all. We (read the church) need to give them time, give them room, and God will use their story in His time, in His way, according to His purpose.

Diana Ventura, an AIDS researcher for Harvard University, authored *Our Fractured Wholeness*, a book from which I quote frequently. Having grown up with cerebral palsy, unable to play with other children, and often being laughed at because of it, she is intimately familiar with the spectrum of brokenness and its concomitant suffering. For her, those who have been broken by life often find it easier to connect with God because they are more in touch with reality and have less pride that prevents them from admitting their brokenness and need for God. As she puts it,

> When we accept our brokenness, our fractured lives are no longer an avenue for pain, but something far more remarkable—a conduit for intimacy with God. And if we are willing to venture into the depths of our pain to act faithfully, God teaches us the divine lessons that grow through the cracks of our fragmented beings and bodies.[27]

On the matter of the "softer side of ministry," to include the less overt witnesses among us, a former friend from a church I once attended literally freaked out because I recommended the movie *The Shack*. He got so ugly about it that I ended up having to block him on social media because he relentlessly pursued me day and

---

[27] Diana Ventura, *Our Fractured Wholeness: Making the Courageous Journey from Brokenness to Love* (Eugene, OR: Cascade Books, 2010), 47.

night trying to get me to denounce it as heretical. Why? Because in the movie, based on the bestselling book, a black woman was portrayed as God the Father, called Papa (gasp!), a middle Eastern man was Jesus (the only "normal" role of the Godhead), and an Asian woman named Sarayu was the Holy Spirit (gasp!). The movie broaches the horrific subject of child murder with an implication of molestation. Mack, the child's father, himself was abused, and he and his wife previously had lost another child. How do you tackle a subject like that in any kind of straightforward way and plan to help people cope with such inconceivably complicated trauma, loss, and grief? Fictional role playing was how, and for me and most others it was genius.

Too many evangelicals are too hard edged and concrete; things are either black or white, good or bad, right or wrong. I know because I used to be one until I learned better. Life is simple for them and being subtle is being wishy-washy, weak-kneed, namby-pamby, or watered down. As a prison chaplain, I was involved with most of the family losses among the unit's population, which amounted to an almost daily part of my work, sometimes half a dozen in a day.

One mother, claiming to be a school guidance counselor, adamantly demanded the right to tell her daughter about her grandmother's passing herself. I suggested that she let us do that, to make sure she would be safe (some throw themselves onto the floor; some need medical help with the spike in stress), for which we were well practiced and trained, and then she could have a better visit once the inmate was over the initial shock. All to no avail; it was like talking to proverbial bricks.

Acquiescing to the woman's demands, we arranged a private place away from normal visitation. As soon as her daughter arrived, the mother launched into her monologue, telling her the news, telling her how to feel about it, how to act about it, telling her not to cry, and laying out each and every step for the near future, and only then was she finished. The daughter barely spoke, but the mother didn't even seem to notice.

Later, in my office, when she was allowed space to grieve and not be directed about what to do, feel, think, or say, she talked freely about her grandmother, which was visibly cathartic for her. Other times, those in my office with losses would cry uncontrollably, or just weep quietly, or just sit and rock in their chair, wiping their tears. I never discouraged any reaction to such news; for me, there is no wrong way to react or process grief and loss. The above woman's mother could not have done a worse job; she literally did every single thing wrong in that situation. I'm sure she loved her daughter, but she didn't have a clue about how to handle loss and grief, despite being self-convinced she was an expert.

I'm confident that God handled the "heresy" of *The Shack* quite handily because He knows just how many families, friends, and relatives of affected families and friends needed this specific kind of ministry that isn't easily found in most traditional forms. And I believe He also inspired the blend of fact and fiction, of pure evil cast within subtle creativity at its most sensitive. This courageous movie tackled the most serious of subjects with master's level nuancing—a difference only the wise learn in real life—and it accomplished something that I don't think any other means would have.

The Shack ministered to an incalculable wound; it gently brought light to an excruciating pain—not just one horrific loss but several. It softly and smoothly delivered God's love uniquely through each person of the novel trinity. The net effect was a well-coordinated, thorough spiritual balm, a holistic body, mind, and soul type of intensive care, which allowed a peace that arguably might never have come to Mack and his family by other means. If someone ever brings such a disaster to you, please do not use scriptural Band-aids. Instead, what about just listening and caring without trying to fix the unfixable? Whatever you do, please don't *ever* say, "God must have needed another angel." We have two ears and one mouth for good reason. Start with stopping talking; start with simply listening, which is neither simple nor easy. You cannot fix grief, so let God minister His peace through your caring, *quiet* presence.

The quote below is from a synopsis of the movie, which captures only a small portion, but notice the prevalence of this book's theme, which could only be expressed in a fictional context:

> Sarayu touches Mack's eyes so that he can see as the three of them see. When he opens his eyes, Mack finds himself on a small hill overlooking a clearing. The world glimmers with light emanating from every living creature. The clearing fills with a group of children glowing with inner white light, and then a circle of adults shining with more complicated colors, and finally a circle of angels glowing blue.[28]

---

[28] William P. Young, "The Shack Summary," Lit Charts, https://www.litcharts.com/lit/the-shack/summary.

The Shack wasn't any more heresy than children playing Joseph and Mary and saying silly things that make everyone laugh. It wasn't any more heresy than rock 'n roll music in church.[29] Lighten up, my harsh, hard-headed, black-and-white, zero-gray friends. Let God expand your thinking, and with it He will expand you in so many other ways. The following is from a book I read while preparing for a sermon titled "Stranger Danger!" It was about how we all have lists of "strangers" with whom we choose not to associate, or worse exclude through either overt or unconscious bias:

> the biblical word for hospitality is *philoxenia, Philia* . . . the Greek word for brotherly love. Hospitality begins in the heart ... Christians are called to extend *philia* to strangers ... that hospitality—welcoming God in strangers and seeing Jesus in disguise—begins by *widening the circle of our affections, the circumference of our care, the arena of our compassion, and the territory of our kindness.*[30]

The precious phrases, "widening the circle, the circumference, the arena, and the territory ... of our affections, care, compassion, and kindness" have become a set of guiding lights for me, an ongoing inspiration whenever I am challenged to serve and love those who are difficult to serve and love. Even as a prison chaplain who was used to being around scary looking characters and bad actors, by applying this principle, I often found them to be quite human indeed,

---

[29] When it was new, the majority of traditional church folks reacted with great disdain, even saying that Christian rock music came straight from the Devil.

[30] Richard Beck, *Stranger God: Meeting Jesus in Disguise* (Minneapolis: Fortress Press, 2017), Kindle loc. 102, emphasis added.

and sometimes they had delightful hearts. Sometimes, the scariest among them were the humblest, the most receptive to God's love and grace, and the most passionate when it came time to share their faith.

I remember one quite well, a pretty, shy woman with quite a few tattoos, who hadn't been taking care of herself and had a gruff exterior—a piece of armor with which I was familiar. I fully understood the distrust of people trampling around in her pain-filled world. I was going to need patience. Over time, when she eventually realized she could trust me, she began to open up, telling me about her early years as a child actress. But there was a big problem in the home, namely her grandfather who was sexually abusing her on a regular basis. She ran away from home at age 9 because living on the street was safer than being at home. Is it any wonder that she became promiscuous, became an addict, and ended up in prison? Even there, she still suffered the throes of addiction, acquiring other inmates' pills by any means possible, and often suffering severe medical reactions. Her life was a tragedy somewhat like the girl in *The Shack*, but she survived (and Mack was a good father). I do believe that over the months I knew her she improved and absorbed some of the essence of my caring work with her. One thing I know is that had I not been gentle to the utmost and willing to listen, she wouldn't have heard a word from me much less shared cathartically from her heart.

As we learn to manage this powerful light within, we acquire wisdom about not applying it recklessly or harshly, which caution comes naturally to us since we already know all too well just how quickly kindness can be taken advantage of and go sideways. We are well versed in being burned, but this also gives us great insight to know when we are applying light well, with great care, and appropriately. Thus, we've learned well, and we're wise as serpents but harmless as doves (Matt. 10:16). We know much about life's harsh consequences for the naive, but we learned over time how to maneuver around such obstacles because the mission of light carrying, light ministering, and light healing are far too important to be deterred.

Our inner light is portable because it is meant to be shared, given away, and to drive out the darkness—of which nothing else is qualified or capable. The light is also sensitive to eyes held too long in the dark, who need less right or wrong and good and bad, less "just pray harder," and more "how are you holding up ... I can't imagine how hard that is ... that's a lot for anyone to handle." It's one thing to share our heavenly light with others stumbling around in the dark, and it's quite another to blast them with high beams like stereotypical redneck pickups with mounted rows of hunting spotlights. So many B-movies movies have been made about such blinding LEDs and the fear they can inflict riding the bumpers of innocent, terrorized drivers.

It's one thing to share the truth; it's another to beat someone up with it. I've met some of this type, and somehow in their minds that's the only way—and they justify it all day long. I'm sure everyone has had bosses and supervisors like this—inflexible, one-track mind, emotional IQ set on deaf, can't read a room or a person, won't listen and can't learn, just pedal to the metal clubbing others with what they decide they need to hear, and hear it they will—yet they can't hear 2 Timothy.

The raw truth is they are ineffective at best, obnoxious at worst, like hunter spotlights in your face, often doing more harm than good, and sometimes causing brand new damage to already damaged hearts. This has nothing to do with whether they are speaking true things or not. I'm reminded of a very funny Saturday Night Live episode, "The Sensitive Drill Sergeant."[31] Ironically, they push people away from the light instead of drawing them toward it. That makes them stumbling blocks and harsh overlords, ill advised by both the OT and NT (Prov. 15:1; 1 Cor. 8:9).

Two of the best things I learned in CPE[32] were 1) the "ministry of presence" and 2) how to listen and how not to. Once, a visibly stressed inmate came to my office needing to talk with me. She was going through quite a major crisis in her life, the details of which I don't remember, but I do recall well what she said at the end of the session. She thanked me with sincere gratitude for taking the time to speak with her. I hadn't said more than a few words to her, but she just needed someone to listen while she unloaded, not unlike how we do with God. Sometimes, just being there is enough.

Have you ever met that person who "listens" by saying on the heels of every few words, "mm-*hmm*," "mm-*hmm*," "mm-*hmm*"? They are listening to respond, not to understand. They can't wait for you to stop talking so they can start. The above freight train "guidance counselor" is another prime example, along

---

[31] SNL, "The Sensitive Drill Sergeant," Season 24, 1998, https://www.youtube.com/watch?v=0X5xql1G4QY. Worth the watch!

[32] Clinical Pastoral Education, a formal, usually fulltime program for training chaplains, mostly conducted in large hospitals.

with the classic "fix it" syndrome (for those who don't know, fixers can be male or female).

Listening skills are found in many resources, but I highly recommend *Listening Ministry* by Susan Hedahl.[33] If you are ever in a position to speak into others' lives, especially the hurting and broken, take the time to learn some new skills, because they won't simply fall out of the sky or happen while you sleep. Then watch God minister with His presence in their spirits ... and hold your tongue when they dare to share their pain.

My brother Karl shares a relevant story from his time as a pastor when he was on vacation in Europe:

"Early in my ministry we were traveling in Germany, driving a rented car, trying to navigate in a country where we didn't speak the language. One day we parked curbside and visited a shop in downtown Dresden. When we came out the car wouldn't start. I tried everything I knew to try, including opening the hood and staring at the engine as if the problem would be evident to me. Soon a man who was sitting at an outdoor cafe came over, looked at the engine with me and said something that sounded like, 'Ah-Day-Ah-Tse.' I tried to explain that I didn't speak German, and I didn't understand what he was saying. I tried pointing to the battery, the wiring, and he kept repeating the exact same German word, only a little louder each time.

"Eventually he was shouting very loudly, and I was just laughing. After about ten minutes of this he gave up

---

[33] Susan K. Hedahl, *Listening Ministry: Rethinking Pastoral Leadership* (Minneapolis: Fortress Press, 2001).

and went back to drinking his beer. I spotted a well-dressed young man carrying a briefcase and I asked if he spoke English. He did and agreed to come stare at the engine with me. After a moment he said, 'Ah-Day-Ah-Tse.' Oh brother, I thought, here we go again. Then he told me in English that Ah-Day-Ah-Tse is the German form of AAA. We went to a nearby pay phone (this was before cell phones), he called ADAC and told me they would send someone right out. Then he said he would stay with us until the car was running again! We enjoyed our twenty minutes together, talking about our travels, him helping with directions and suggestions to make our trip more pleasant. Soon we were on our way.

"Driving to our next stop, I thought how the first guy knew what we needed and tried to communicate it to us in ever louder terms that we could not understand. But he wasn't willing to actually do anything to help. I wondered how often we do that in our preaching ministry, just say the same things louder and louder to people who have no idea what we are talking about. The second man also knew what we needed, actually did something to get us help, and then he practiced the vitality important ministry of presence. He took the time to listen to us and spoke to us in language we could understand.

"Both preaching and presence are necessary to help those navigating a strange world. We need to learn to balance the two and do both."

Francis of Assisi expressed it succinctly when he said, "Preach the Gospel at all times and when necessary, use words."

5. Light as Being and Identity

Identity seems to be a universal problem in today's world. Young people especially seem to struggle with it like never before. Each generation, of course, has its own unique problems with the subject, but the question of "Who am I?" seems to loom larger than life today, like the great Oz on the big, deafening screen of youthful minds. It affects adults as well, perhaps also in greater numbers, but mostly it's a burning matter for callow souls who are still developing but who feel pressure to make certain life-altering decisions *immediately*.

They're not given time to think, reason, or work things out in their own time and way. They're not even to consider consulting adults, parents, or "old" people, much less those out of touch, obsolete, spiritual advisors who cling to their antiquated Bibles. In some places, laws have been put in place specifically to prevent parents from learning the indoctrination *du jour*. It's like the enemy of our souls is turning up all the burners; it's like the most pressurized full court press of the ages. He's pulling out all the stops with a full-frontal assault on the tender senses of the tender aged. I envision his pitch as something like this, "Don't you really want to be *this*? What's stopping you? Why wait? Decide *now*! *Everyone else* knows what they want! What if you don't decide and you're *never* happy? Go with your *feelings*!"

It's no longer about "Who do I want to be when I grow up?" or "What do I want to do when I get out of school or college?" It starts much younger, and it comes with unbelievable peer pressure to conform to the "*new* norm," which suddenly is the "*only* norm." This, of course, is happening simultaneously—the oldest strategy in the oldest war books, a two-pronged attack—with an all-out assault on traditional values, conservative principles, and especially anything related to the word Christian. We, of course, are all "Nazis" who want nothing but *control,* and all of it comes from hearts full of *hate* and *fear*—I mean, *everyone* knows this, right? And like so many fish gulping down the tastiest worms, an entire generation seems to be on an oblivious feeding frenzy.

The tyranny of the urgent and the loudest voice in the room temporarily drown out the quieter, gentler, wiser voice of the ages, the one whose "pick up line" has never changed or wavered—"I love you. I always have. I always will. I forgive you. Come home." Sure, people of all ages have always had and will always have this same choice—unless a competitor for souls has his own agenda for overpowering that message (time-sensitive perhaps, as in running out of it?), at which time the heat is turned up to the max in a fast and furious offensive.

I'm reminded of countless women for decades being sold the "it's only a bunch of cells" line but never being honestly informed, much less allowed to see the ultrasound showing quite clearly a complete, tiny human being; and, *of course*, never being shown the reconstruction on a tray afterward to make sure no parts were missed—in short, both straight out lied to and lied to by omission, thus never given a *real* choice by the so-called healthcare professionals.[34]

When there's only one option available, and it's a matter of life or death if you don't decide *right now*, it's a pitch, a ruse, a grift, a hustle. The youth are being bamboozled, swindled, and scammed. After all, who can argue with your *identity*? After all, it's all about *your* body, *your* feelings, *your* choices, *your* rights … and of course, every grade-schooler and high-schooler already knows everything that matters about everything in life—starting with the fact that they are at the very center of the known universe! Having grown up literally having to sniff roadkill before being forced to take it home for dinner, the phrase "if it doesn't smell right, it probably isn't" carries both personal and timeless wisdom.

So that's today's "catch" line, the "gotcha'" moment when the agenda drivers know the game has worked? Make it about *identity*, make it *urgent*, make it the *only*

---

[34] See the movie *Unplanned* for an inside look at the industry by a woman who ran Houston's biggest Planned Parenthood clinic for eight years. Abby Johnson, Chuck Konzleman, and Gary Solomon, *Unplanned* (Pure Flix Entertainment, 2019),
https://www.imdb.com/title/tt9024106/plotsummary/?ref_=tt_ov_pl.

choice, and keep hammering away at any and all dissenting "Nazi" voices. Because the puppet masters are trained to never vary from the script, this is perhaps the greatest con that's ever been foisted in the history of cons. Think about it—master manipulators are being trained and sent out to con your children, the younger the better—and you're ostracized from the process.

Ah, but like they have throughout history, once again they greatly underestimate the power of the calmer, more powerful voice, the one who only ever speaks of love, forgiveness, peace, joy, truth, freedom, light. Right along with the tide of the freshly snookered, now gasping for air like so many landed fish, is another surging tide— those who, instead of wormy hooks, have ingested a never-ending feast of goodness, a veritable eternity of the best of the best, served by the Master Chef and Creator of every good gift. What? A *better* identity? How is this possible? Yes, a better identity. A true identity, without pressure, without catches, without gotchas, and without lies of omission or any other kind.

The quieter voice reminds about being created in the image of the creator, about being formed in His likeness, captured with sublime language like *imago dei*. It's the way and nature of light—to spread the wealth, and each replication is entirely a new offspring of the parent light, whole lights in their own right; whole as in inherited, each fully and uniquely *imago dei*—permanent identities.

That's the answer to those being pressured to conform to the "new, improved" identity—because *imago dei* is our only true identity, no matter what the trickster-in-chief or his mantra-chanting minions claim.

Truth isn't relative and never has been. Truth is truth and all other versions are some kind of con. There is only one truth, and that truth has been truth from the beginning. That truth became flesh, and that truth walked among us and made true claims—"I am the way, the truth, and the life. I am the light of the world. I am the only one who loves you eternally. I always have, and I always will. I forgive you. Wake up and see the light of truth." There's a difference between being woke and being awake. Wake up, sleeper, your light has come!

In 2004, Diane Sawyer grilled Mel Gibson hard about his new movie, *The Passion of the Christ*, pressuring him every which way to admit it was anti-Semitic. He calmly replied, "It's all there in black and white, Diane. Read it for yourself."[35] She kept citing those "with questions," who "were concerned." To the spiritually blind, the Bible is whatever they want it to be, like it doesn't even matter—you take your truth from it; I'll take mine. What difference does it make? And if they have power and position, like a media personality, they come at folks with all the pressuring passion they can muster, however blind they might actually be to guide anyone anywhere.

It's up to God's people to point to His message that never wavers: "Let us make man in our own image, after our likeness" (Gen. 1:26)—made in the image (Hebrew, *d'mut*); after the likeness (Hebrew, *serem*). In the New Testament, "He is the *image* of the invisible God" (Greek, *eikon*). Made of the same nature, the same DNA, the same truth, the same light. Jesus was the *eikon* of God, and we also were made in the *eikon* of God and are

---

[35] "Mel Gibson's *Passion*: Primetime Live Interview with Diane Sawyer" (2004): https://www.youtube.com/watch?v=7Ecnfe530IE.

43

being remade into that *eikon*: "and have put on the new self, which is being renewed in knowledge after the image [*eikon*] of its creator" (Col. 3:10).

Maybe instead of condemning the deceptive message, we simply offer a better one? Maybe instead of trying to turn up the heat and compete head on like crashing rams, we turn the heat down, take the pressure off— make it okay to take your time and not rush into surgery, so to speak (or literally). Make it okay get a second opinion; what could it hurt? Like so many other Moms, mine always said, "You attract more flies with honey than vinegar." It's the same with finnicky, fragile fledglings who are suddenly confused about things like identity and "who they are"—besides, they have to decide all this *right now* or their life won't be worth living!

Those who truly love them know that confusion always comes from the confuser-in-chief, who has turned up the confusion volume like never before. So, attract them with their true identity. No shouting needed. Just simple straight truth, simple love, pure light. Something inside will hear the truth even if there is no response in the moment, because truth always rings true, and light always dispels darkness. Have you looked behind yourself, honey? What's that big bright light standing right there? How long has he been there? Wait, what's that he's saying?

> Come, child, let's have a chat. Yeah, you've done some stupid things (and won some stupid prizes). Yeah, you've been a hot mess and then some. Yeah, you're damaged in so many sad ways. I'm not here to dwell on all that. I'm here to forgive and love and

offer peace and truth and light. I'm here so you can start over and live your original identity—you know, the one I created within you. I've known you since that first spark of life, since you were being knit together … deep down, you know who I am, and you know I'm speaking the truth. And deep down, you know I'm the only one who loves you just the way you are. You're mine is who you are.

Here's a fascinating fact that I first heard from my pastor in a sermon and then verified through research. Apparently, there is an actual flash of light at the moment of conception, which has a scientific explanation about millions of zinc atoms (below), but also has a spiritual parallel. If we are made in the image of God, and He is light personified, then it stands to reason at our moment of conception that something like a divine "spark" would occur. The following is from a science journal that published the work of a team of scientists from Northwestern University in Chicago:

> Using a new fluorescent sensor that's able to track the movements of zinc in live cells, the team caught a glimpse of an egg's zinc-storage capabilities, and found some 8,000 zinc compartments, each one containing around 1 million zinc atoms, just ripe for exploding. The tiny "fireworks" that result were found to last for about 2 hours after fertilization.[36]

---

[36] Science Alert, "Scientists Just Captured the Flash of Light that Sparks when a Sperm Meets an Egg" (April 27, 2016), https://www.sciencealert.com/scientists-just-captured-the-actual-flash-of-light-that-sparks-when-sperm-meets-an-egg. **I highly recommend watching the video; the still frame barely captures it.**

The article includes a short movie depicting the creation of new life as more like fireworks than a spark (the red dot is a sperm; the blue circle is an egg), with the zinc atoms surrounding the egg in a micro explosion of light. As with many questions to which we'll never have the answers, this evidence generated a lot of debate, but my response is "Why wouldn't He?" If we're out to debunk God at every turn, then of course we will protest. If we believe God is light and His word is truth, then we have no reason to object. Why wouldn't he create each new life in exactly this magnificent way?

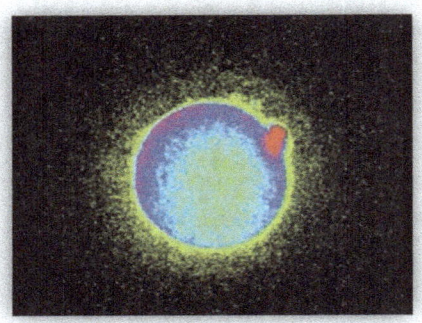

Here's another thought. If God creates a visible light show at the conception of physical life, I have to wonder about the parallel process with the conception of new spiritual life. The phrase "born again" uses two specific Greek words, *gennao*, meaning normal birth, and *anothen*, meaning "from above." We are first born physically and then we have a second birth, this time born again from above. I literally asked the same question as Nicodemus in John 3:4, "How can a person be born when he is old? He cannot enter his mother's womb a second time and be born, can he?" It was a snarky question, tainted with habitual sarcasm, but it was reflective of the cognitive dissonance the statement inherently carries.

The understanding came soon enough, and I've been trying to put it into words ever since for others also blinded and broken by the darkness. So, when the spiritual lights come on at the moment of salvation, I believe there is an equivalent explosion that we alone can see as our souls are suddenly illuminated by the very presence of God. Isn't it just like God to do such an amazing thing, at both our physical and spiritual conceptions? I might not have been able to put it into words had I not seen the physical version in the video.

The same principle of "why wouldn't God do it" applies to other discoveries, such as finding an intact, nearly complete scroll of Isaiah in 1947 at Qumran, Israel.[37] Why wouldn't Jesus commit the exact scroll—from which He just read, personally having fulfilled its prophecy about His mission—to be preserved for modern discovery two millennium later?

I've had the fortune to see the original Qumran Isaiah scroll at the Shrine of the Book exhibit in the Israel Museum in Jerusalem prior to it being swapped for a copy since the light was slowly  damaging it. Despite being instructed not to, I was an overeager tourist who couldn't resist the temptation to take this photo. I've also had the privilege of seeing one of a handful of complete, 33 ft. long copies that exist in

---

[37] History of Information, "The Great Isaiah Scroll: The Only Nearly Complete Biblical Book Surviving Among the Dead Sea Scrolls," https://www.historyofinformation.com/detail.php?id=143.

the world, which is on display at the Lanier Theological Library in Spring, TX.[38]

One final thought along the same lines. . . why wouldn't Jesus leave an imprint of His face on His grave cloth when He was resurrected from the dead? If there is an explosion of light at conception, and our souls are illuminated by heaven at our second birth, it only makes sense that Jesus' resurrection would involve a light powerful enough to leave an imprint—in a real sense, brilliant enough to expose the first photographic negative on a simple piece of cloth.[39] His appearance wasn't a secret while recently alive, so why wouldn't He show His face this way for the benefit of those who would never get to see Him in person in this life?

We live in a time when the deceiver-in-chief is busy casting doubt about every single truth that has ever existed, but we also have an even greater and growing plethora of evidence confirming and supporting the historical reality of our great God and Father, His creation, and His Word. The simple truth is we have no excuse but to see Him everywhere we look (Rom. 1:20). We derived our original, physical identity from Him, born with His image in our DNA, we have been born again into His marvelous light (1 Pet. 2:9), and we look forward to our own resurrection to come (2 Cor. 4:14). We are who He says we are—we are His children, born with His image, and born again into His light.

---

[38] Lanier Theological Library and Learning Center, https://lanierlibraryandlearningcenter.org.

[39] Britannica, "Shroud of Turin," https://www.britannica.com/topic/Shroud-of-Turin.

6. A Kinder, Gentler Light

A saying I found that fits this material seamlessly says, "A heart full of kindness glows different." I happen to believe that the kindest souls have seen the most pain, which has created a metamorphosis within them, so they want to ensure that, for their entire lives, they never intentionally inflict pain on others—quite the opposite. Kahlil Gibran penned, "Out of suffering have emerged the strongest souls; the most massive characters are seared with scars." From experience and having met many of those characters, I would add that suffering also produces the kindest and the most caring souls.

When some of us crash landed on life's bottom and experienced our personal worst brokenness, it was the only way we would have heard the wake-up call at all. Only then did we realize the only way out was up, which meant the way to freedom was to fly, which meant cocooning, growing wings in a place of confinement, and then finally stretching out our new, awkward but transcendent wings. Only then did we launch our first flight into our new life, winging our way heavenward.

Our suffering is never wasted because we learned early on in life that there were small seeds of grace and wisdom hidden within the bitter, hard shells of sorrow. During these times, when our eyes were being pried open with crowbars as it were, it dawned on us that it was in the falling, breaking, and disintegration that the brilliance of the master plan was being revealed. Seeds have to die to produce life (1 Cor. 15:36); likewise, souls often have to be broken and buried, and sometimes crash and burn, to produce new life. For some, that's a metaphorical death; for others, it's a literal screaming nosedive and fiery explosion. But then, Sunday comes!

The surviving golden embers among the ashes are the reconstituted parts that now have a new mission. This time, life won't ever be the same; this time, we will live better—we will be kinder, gentler, and we will readily share this new, glowing, scar light rather than hoarding it like whatever little we previously had would be scraped together and miserly rationed. This time, we find that we seem to have a never-ending supply of oil for our radiant, bright candle, and the things we once craved, fought, and scrapped over—tiny bits and scraps of peace and joy—suddenly seem to have a bottomless supply.

People like to glibly quote, "Whatever doesn't break you will make you stronger," which I always thought was trite until I became broken, and the breaking made me stronger in all those exact places. Once we've gone through the dying/rising process, and we are given the honor of serving, we are given both a mission and the gifts and equipment we will need for the journey— especially things like discipline, humility, the strength of a darkness survivor, and an orientation of someone who isn't always looking out for #1 (1 Pet. 5:1-14).

On that subject, a personal pet peeve of mine is folks who are always talking about the "five-fold gifts of the Spirit," as if to say, "I got mine; what did you get?" Maybe it's my broken hearing, but the unspoken along with that seems to say, "Too bad for you that you didn't get what I got. Maybe someday if you get to be spiritual like me, you'll get something better." I've heard the above short list quoted from scripture until I couldn't stand to hear it anymore. Some with the previously mentioned, black-and-white thinking seem to act like this is it—here's the list; you're either included or you're not. If not, sorry for you; you might try praying harder.

In real life, however, this kind of thing never seemed so clearly and neatly defined. I have known people who had the gift of smiling, for example, even though it's not on any official list. They effortlessly light up every room they enter; it's a free gift to give cheer to anyone and everyone. I once had a Chapel worker like that, literally always smiling, and I often wondered how she managed, knowing well her daily suffering. Others I've known with something from the official list have had sour faces, like their gifts had negative effects on their humorless personalities, almost like smiling or joking were frowned upon. I've also known people with the gift of calm, able to maintain in any chaos; or of empathy, always caring about others, always ready to listen, for whom life is never all about them—again, given away freely with no expectation of anything in return. Yet again, missing from the official list.

I have always wanted to be around gifted people like these and to learn how to emulate them, the smilers, the unrattled, the empathizers, the listeners, and so many like them. I've known people with the gift of wisdom—knowing when to speak and when not to, with all the courage and serenity of the famous prayer. Who doesn't like to be around calm, brave, smiling, wise, caring people like these? Yet, those with the "important" gifts can seem dismissive of such folks at times; after all, it's not like they have official titles, so that puts them at a lower level, right? Not that anyone would ever say that out loud, of course. But they might act like it.

At the same time, scripture also talks about the fruits of the Spirit. Now that is something I can wrap my head around. I may not have a single official gift, but I can develop at least some of these many delectable fruits. As one professor friend succinctly put the lofty aspiration of Gal. 5:22-25 on the bottom shelf, "I can be kind to you … I can be patient with you … I can be gentle with you." It's not a "you've either made the grade or you haven't" kind of thing; it's nothing whatsoever to do with official or unofficial. It's something that the Spirit works into us a little at a time; it's the inner work of a lifetime to practice and polish until different parts begin to emerge naturally—but they're all available now to practice on and start growing. Who doesn't like a joyful person? Who except the sour faces doesn't appreciate someone with a sense of humor? Who doesn't like a peaceful person, or someone who can suffer with you as long as needed, or someone whose presence and words are like healing medicine to your raw parts? I'm reminded of an old Amy Grant song with the line, "Show your daddy where it hurts."[40]

Something tells me there is too much pride and ego involved with being too ready to claim as many official gifts as possible, the titles and prestige that go with them, the big chairs (and sometimes big hair) ... and the off-putting attitudes they too often evoke. I have to question those who insist on multiple attributes or adjectives by their name: "The Most Holy Anointed Reverend Apostle" ... and the like. Simultaneously, I believe there is a common denominator whenever we see someone exhibiting the fruits of the Spirit, which is humility. You can be a teacher, preacher, or evangelist and still have quite a large ego. But unless you're a master faker, you can't exhibit the fruits of the Spirit without humility. The best part is fruit isn't even for the fruit bearers; it's always existed for everyone else's pleasure and nurture.

I've shared often that orange trees don't crank out oranges for themselves; it's always for others. Grapefruit trees don't grunt and struggle and strive to produce their tasty fruit ... they just have to stay connected and let God do the work of supplying and producing the bountiful crops (John 15:4; 2 Cor. 9:10). Next thing you

---

[40] Amy Grant, "Lay Down" (the Burden of Your Heart), My Father's Eyes (1979), https://genius.com/Amy-grant-lay-down-the-burden-of-your-heart-lyrics.

know, out pops a fruit, and then another until the tree is full and all the neighbors share in the abundance. In contrast, you might have to work hard to achieve a gift, and sometimes the striving can be strong among those who desire it greatly. In truth, as an immature Christian, I once strived for a certain title, and I was quite upset when it wasn't given to me. What a humbling revelation when I finally realized the reason God kept it from me— it had been about me, not Him. Ironically, as I learned instead to focus on fruit, the titles came naturally.

A poet named Mona Lisa Nyman wrote, "If you could see all the light you've brought into this world, you'd never have a single moment of doubt about your worth ever again." Don't let the spiritual ladder climbers and long title holders make you either envious of them or discourage you from your passionate pursuit of the most beautiful parts of life in the Spirit.

Ironically, the gifts require the most humility to be done for His glory, and too many are doing it for their own glory. The fruit, on the other hand, is all about becoming like Him, the One who teaches them day by day about becoming calm, smilers, givers, carers, listeners, and wise ones—to whom others go when they need to hear from Him, when their souls need healing words and the uplifting medicine of hope and light.

As they grow these fruits, they also learn how to love and serve selflessly, with all the humility of a King who left His throne far behind, thinking nothing of it, then humbling himself, washing his subject's feet, and then suffered as they suffered, willingly sacrificing everything for them (Phil. 2:6-8).

7. Light's Healing Touch

A long time ago, I was a struggling freelance writer who took on a few assignments for a charismatic magazine for a time. I was sent to an event featuring a faith healer, who was dressed in white from head to toe, and where I was seated in the front row since I was a "very important person." What that vantage point gave me was a closeup of the act of healing, which afterward seemed an appropriate description; at least, that was my conclusion. Maybe I'm a skeptic about such things; maybe I lack faith. I've just never been a fan of falling backwards on demand, and even if I were ever "slain," I can't imagine I would be chewing gum on my back.

For the longest time, the subject of healing was a sore spot for me at worst and a challenge at best. Maybe it's because too many tried to fix my sordid, twisted life with Bible Band-aids and bumper sticker theology—

"just pray harder," "just forgive and forget," "just don't dwell on it." Granted, I didn't make it easy for them, even though they all surely had the very best of intentions and sincere hearts. Thankfully, my faith grew over time, along with a few pearls of wisdom coating the irritation, and I began to see that healing is rarely something simple or straightforward. I began to understand that it's more gradual, like something I learned in seminary called "the hermeneutical spiral"[41]— immerse yourself in the word, take what you glean out into the world, return with life lessons in hand, immerse yourself again, and so on, creating an ever-expanding spiral of knowledge and growth.

Of course, I'd be foolish to throw shade on all those who have been instantly and miraculously healed—there are far too many medically verified stories; far too many circumstances that are far beyond coincidental. What I'm opposed to is healing on demand, like the Holy Spirit is just going to show up at 7:30 pm because the healer has to produce for the camera. The other type is the above well-intentioned person who cares and wants to help but realizes they are out of their depth, but rather than being humble about it and kneeling down alongside the sufferer praying for help, they forge ahead with disingenuous confidence and spout tacky quips that sound religious but simply are not helpful.

In my experience, the layered process of healing deep trauma can take a considerable amount of time. Think of all the things that got destroyed along the way, for example, with the child model mentioned earlier—trust,

---

[41] Grant Osborne, *The Hermeneutical Spiral: A Comprehensive Introduction to Biblical Interpretation* (Downers Grove: IVP Academic, 2006).

confidence, healthy sense of self, natural joy, innocence, and much more. Think of all the things that were simultaneously denied—love, normalcy, healthy routines, laughter, fun, freedom, support, safety, exploration, and much more. Add years of surviving on the streets, and mix in several addictions, some random new traumas, and then bring in the above advisor to say, "Just forgive and forget. Just don't dwell on it. Just pray harder."

As a rule, if your moment of ministry starts with the word "just," you're already missing the mark. I can't even count how many times I heard these very words, which is why I became allergic to them. Why was everyone afraid to say, "Let's face it, you've got a lot of hard work ahead of you; every moment of progress is going to require painful honesty, and you're often going to want to run the other way because you don't want or think you need any more pain, but that's the nature of healing." Whether severe burns from a fire or multiple broken bones from a car accident, healing usually hurts, healing usually takes time, and healing is almost never instant. And no one can manipulate the Holy Spirit.

In my case, healing started with quite a rude awakening. I knew I was beyond broken, but worse, I didn't believe it was even possible to be put back together—I just knew I was a goner, a real life Humpty Dumpty. When I finally got sober enough to listen to my brother's advice to get help, I ended up arguing for days with a young couple, Mike and Colleen, who had the courage to open a drug rehab place as an outreach mission of their church. One day when I was launching a new round of my daily ignorance, Colleen stopped me, looked me in the eyes, and said matter-of-factly, "Kevin, you're blind." Even the very first step of healing hit me, as the Brits say, "like the proverbial hitting the fan." I was speechless for a change, surely much to her relief. God got to me in that sacred moment of hard truth, in which instant time was suspended while the Spirit penetrated my heart of hearts with the burning, piercing sword of light that cured my blindness in a single surgical stroke. It's true that "I saw the light" for the first time, but it was hardly a pain-free experience.

Even then, reeling as it were and still on step one after my personal lightning bolt from the blue, I wasn't anywhere near fully healed. This was just the first of a seemingly endless wave of visits to the great Physician's Office for inner surgeries, and the Carpenter's Shop for more renovations,[42] stretching across decades, each addressing the most critical issue at the time. My heart was still a tangled ball of scars, and while I finally had inner peace and joy, much of me still remained in need of His healing touch. In fact, I don't think the divine intent is to return us to a pristine state, to make all the broken parts disappear. My life verse is "He makes all things new" (2 Cor. 5:17), which is inclusive of our spiritual rebirth and the opening of our eyes, but also the gradual removal of our old selves, which spanning a lifetime becomes the present progressive, "I am making all things new" (Rev. 21:5)." Following Jesus' own example, I don't think our scars vanish at our personal resurrection, and I believe that is by intentional design.

---

[42] See Kevin Hrebik, *The Carpenter's Shop and Other Metaphors* (Amazon: KDP, 2022). The cover comes from the same reconstructed Nazareth village as mentioned in Chapter 3.

We aren't perfected when we receive Jesus into our hearts—we are forgiven, justified, adopted, and so much more, but our saved souls still reside in human bodies, with human histories, and human damage that doesn't all disappear upon light entering our souls and being born again. We still hurt, and we still hurt each other. We still bleed, we still have regrets, we still trip, fall, stumble, and sin. True, we now know we are going to heaven when we die, but we still have a long way to go—we're going to blow it time and again, we're going to make mistakes we'll regret for life, and we're going to move in and out of relationships, careers, homes, and ministries—often leaving a trail of tears behind us, and more often than not, weeping as we lurch forward (2 Pet. 1:5-7).

Famous for his book *The Wounded Healer*, Henri Nouwen wrote that our pain shows us how to "live in connection with the brokenness of humanity."[43] This was the theme of all his writings—solidarity with and empathy for other flawed people also working through the vicissitudes and traumas of life—the good, the bad, and the ugly. In another book, he shared about "signs" from his own wounded, "marked" heart:

> Just as our adulthood shows the *marks* of the struggles of youth, so our solitude bears the *signs* of lonely hours, our care for others reflects at times angry feelings and our prayer sometimes reveals the memory and the presence of many illusions. Transformed in love, however, these painful *signs*

---

[43] Henri J. M. Nouwen, *The Inner Voice of Love: A Journey through Anguish to Freedom* (New York: Doubleday, 1996), 97.

become signs of hope, as the wounds of Jesus did for the doubting Thomas.[44]

From the scars of youthful struggles to the scars of lonely hours, to all the other enduring scars from life's many battles, Nouwen is my personal champion for empathizing with the masses of bruised, battered, and beat down souls. As Jesus said, "The well don't need a physician" (Matt. 9:12); rather, He came for those who did, as He stated Himself about why He came to earth (Luke 4:18). So, for Nouwen, wounded healers come with the same failings as their patients; they speak healing because they are fluent in the vocabulary of suffering ... but their patients might still limp after being healed ... they will still have scars after they are made well ... and most likely, they will still need more healing even after finding inner peace, freedom, and joy. As one person said so well, some have wounds that don't bleed, eyes that don't cry, and hearts that don't feel. Yet Jesus' healing penetrates to our depths and spreads from there.

In another work, *Turn My Mourning into Dancing*, Nouwen shared from experience about the power of hope that can grow in any soil, and how it glows with God's light in the darkest places. In fact, the darker the place, the brighter the light seems to shine. From that book's description, "you too can see how joy and sorrow cannot be separated and how gratitude can help you see everything, even death, in a totally different light."[45]

---

[44] Henri J. M. Nouwen, *Reaching Out: The Three Movements of the Spiritual Life* (New York: Doubleday, 1975), 161–2, emphasis added.

[45] Henri Nouwen, *Turn My Mourning into Dancing: Finding Hope in Hard Times* (Nashville: Thomas Nelson, 2022). From Christianbook.com

8. God's Many Canvases of Light

The above image by Christian artist Thomas Kincaide hangs in my home office. A master painter of light, probably no other modern artist has captured a wider palette of God's infinite variations on the theme. This one depicting a lighthouse next to a cheerfully lit home near a crashing wave is a clear homage to God as our beacon of light in the volatile seas of life, keeping us safe from danger in the darkness.

While they didn't have lighthouses in ancient times, Alexander the Great built a fire tower more than 300 ft. high at the entrance of the Nile. It was named one of the seven wonders of the ancient world. Most of these early forms were simply called beacon fires, but the Romans invented shiny brass mirrors to enhance the flames. One of these, the Tower of Hercules in Spain, is still working.

It wasn't until the 18th century that brighter and more efficient whale oil lamps were created and then state-of-the-art lighting inventions took over. In addition to practical uses, lighthouses became symbolic—of guidance and hope, safety and homecoming, the journey and struggles of life, and the spirit of human endurance and courage.[46] Many still stand as cultural landmarks and inspiration for countless photographers and artists, like Kincaide, and they have been at the center of many tourist attractions and related cottage industries.

What didn't change was the need for lighthouses; indeed, whether primitive or advanced, physical or spiritual, life comes fraught with dangers, especially in its darkest, most dangerous areas. God, of course, is the ultimate lighthouse and source of the original guiding beacon of light and icon of inspiration. His reassuring presence encourages us to persevere in all of life's many storms, trusting that His night vision is clearer than ours, until we at last sail safely into the harbor of rest, there to anchor our souls, per the hymn.

Featured in many of Kincaide's works are sunrises and sunsets, capturing the expansive beauty of not only God's daily handiwork but the endless beauty of light at the hands of the Master Artist. His brilliant displays extend far beyond the capacity of paintbrushes and digital lenses. He paints on the skies and waters, and with equal grandeur creates vivid messages of hope, salvation, and safety on our interior canvases of soul and spirit.

---

[46] Lyndsey Becker, "Lighthouses," Ancient Engineering Marvels (Oct. 18, 2024), https://ancientengineeringmarvels.com/lighthouses-ancient-engineering-marvels/.

Another quote that I keep using comes from the previously mentioned Melissa Kelley, this time finding application in a new context: "God, the Master Artist, is constantly at work in all our lives, bringing hope out of brokenness, in love. All will be well."[47] Where our inner landscapes were often scenes of carnage and devastation, like some kind of lifeless, dystopian world, he enters with new vision, colors, and inspiration—transforming the bleakest and most barren of deserts into life-giving streams of plenty for the redeemed. Once a place of death and dying, now there is everlasting gladness and joy, where sorrow and sighing flee away (Isa. 35:6-10).

God, the eternally compassionate Artist of life ... renovates our interior landscapes and gives us new eyes to see an otherwise hidden world—like C. S. Lewis famously put it, "I believe in Christianity like I believe the sun has risen, not because I see it, but because by it I see everything else."[48] So it is with His entire creation, both things visible and invisible, of which He is both creator and sustainer (Col. 1:16). We can always see Him by the things He has made and abundantly deposited all around us, leaving us without excuse if we remain blind to His handiwork and the truth that He is both Creator and King (Rom. 1:20). How sad indeed are those who are willfully blind and stiff-necked, choosing darkness over light and ignorance over wisdom (John 3:19).

At the time of writing, I was leading a class at my church on the theory of evolution vs. biblical creation. I'm not a scientist but I'm smart enough to trust those

---

[47] Kelley, *Grief: Contemporary Theory*, 141.

[48] C. S. Lewis, "They Asked for a Paper," in *Is Theology Poetry?* (London: Geoffrey Bless, 1962), 164–5.

who are, especially when their conclusions about the data square with scripture. That's the whole difference between the two theories, I've learned, that both are looking at the same data, but they have vastly different interpretations. More than a decade ago, I came across a movie called *Is Genesis History?*[49] and I've been talking, writing, and teaching about it ever since. Compiled by 16 PhDs from every relevant field, they bring the various sciences to life through a biblical worldview. One looks at a T-Rex bone and claims it is 60-70 million years old; another finds flexible tissue inside, and since tissue is a dating method of its own, knows it can't be that old.[50]

This is just one of hundreds of comparative data examples, with one side consistently falling short in the plausibility of its theory's claims. Perhaps the most revealing for me was the mega volcano eruption at Mount St. Helens on May 18, 1980, which recreated the entire landscape for hundreds of miles. The former terrain is now hundreds of feet below the new surface, and the area has regrown most forms of previous life; it looks like it's been there for ages. But this cataclysmic event helped prove God as Creator in multiple ways.

The best part was what happened with Spirit Lake, which was directly below the massive explosion, and the resulting landslide of lava, ash, and rock debris displaced all the water in the lake, depositing layer after layer of the

---

[49] Del Tacket and Thomas Purifoy, *Is Genesis History?* Compass Cinema, 2019. Note that Amazon lists bios of all the contributors.

[50] Mary Schweitzer, Jennifer Whitmeyer, John Horner, and Jan Toporsky, "Soft Tissue Vessels and Cellular Preservation in Tyrannosaurus Rex," *Science* 307, no. 5717 (March 25, 2005): 1952–55, https://science.sciencemag.org/content/307/5717/1952.full. Mentioned by microbiologist Kevin Anderson in *Is Genesis History?*

variegated mudslide, hundreds of feet deep, into the lake. The power of the displaced water scoured a million trees off at the roots of the surrounding valley before being swept back into the lake. As the trees became waterlogged, they started sinking, with the heavier root end going first, then standing vertically at various depths in the mud depending on the type of tree. This layered effect is exactly what is seen at the Grand Canyon with petrified sequoia trees that also have no root ball but are standing at the rim of the canyon at a place called Specimen Ridge. Signs there say it was 50 million years ago, while Mount St. Helens basically happened in a day. It was the same exact effect caused by a cataclysmic event, not millions of years of gradual process. Once again, the data that both sides observe better fits the Bible's flood paradigm.

Without going into all that science here, suffice it to say that the God who paints the skies at sunsets around the world is the original Artist, who created not only the earth but the sun, moon, and stars, who ordered the earth to revolve around the sun, and who created gravity to keep it in place, hanging the earth "on nothing" but space (Job 26:5-14). The oldest book in the Bible talks about what every modern scientist knows today but didn't always know, even just a few centuries ago. The Creator Artist painted the first sunset on a canvas entirely of His creation, which then was a forerunner to every sunset since, until the new earth will come and blow every previous sunset out of the water (Rev. 21:1).

The very same God who created the world also destroyed it by a global flood, which would have been such a catastrophic event that the entire earth's surface, all the way to bedrock, was shifted, dislodged, displaced, utterly recreated by the unimaginable devastation, until every living person, creature, and plant was destroyed, with the sole exception of the people and animals on Noah's Ark. That every major figure in the Bible including Jesus refers to these events and people as historical—collectively more than 200 mentions just in the NT—is not something so easily dismissed just because someone *believes* something else instead of the hard evidence staring them in the face, so to speak.

God is also the same Artist who is busy painting every one of our interior canvases, each a masterpiece in progress. Imagine if we could capture such infinite shades of light and beauty inscribed by our Creator Artist. Imagine if we could express that visibly … what wonders He is in process of capturing, what gems He is busy crafting … and each one carrying a unique spark of the Creator's divine image that someday will be revealed in its entirety, dwarfing even the most breathtaking beauty spread across evening skies through time.

Imagine if humanity had continued to trust God until we had the knowledge to create the science that proved the most basic things, like the fact that the world is round and revolves around the sun. Imagine if we hadn't become arrogant and prideful during the Enlightenment and the Age of Reason eras, when we abandoned God now that we were so far advanced intellectually and scientifically. Imagine the joy that would have spread across the globe had we maintained faith through those (ironically) dark centuries where we removed the now obsolete God from our evolved, *avante-garde* thinking—and then made the discoveries that proved what we used to believe all along by faith. How much brighter and better would the world have been?

This is the work of creationist scientists, who are correcting the errors of the previously deceived and derailed sciences to being back on board with support of rather than denial of scripture. Imagine the great works our collective brains could have accomplished had we not gotten waylaid in the swamps of our own haughty design, mucking about for hundreds of years trying to prove what can't be proven, trying to impose onto the data a paradigm that never did fit, and which even defies logic and science itself. All the opposites fall in place, however, when science simply is unbiased.

As paleontologist Kurt Wise, PhD, asserted: "[After the ice age] the glaciers melted back to their current position, and they are continuing to melt. The thing about global warming; it is warming. The earth is still recovering from the flood."[51] How many generations were ripped off by Darwin's ideas, growing up assuming the charts in biology classrooms were unassailable, scientific fact—missing, as was widely claimed, only a single, final link, which, as was said, was immanently to be found. The problem was it was all a giant deception foisted on an overly trusting population.

Beyond the duping of whole generations came much worse unintended consequences attributed to Darwin in the form of the mass murders of tens of millions via the deadly version of "survival of the fittest." Hitler was inspired and justified by *On the Origin of Species* to purge from the earth the weaker races, helping nature along to

---

[51] *Is Genesis History?* (40:51).

refine a master race. The same inspiration fell on Stalin's ears and spread to most modern age dictators who committed even worse atrocities in the name of Socialism and Communism.[52] All claimed Darwin roots.

Imagine learning as an adult that you had been lied to your whole life. They weren't just missing a single link— *all the links are missing.* There hasn't been a single one found; all that's been hailed as species jumping "evidence" are merely adaptations within species, easily seen as Creator God installing the ability within the various species to adjust to environment and climate. But only whole species are found in the fossil record— no animals in process of "transitioning"—not one.

If evolution is true, there should be limitless "gray areas" in the record, all jumbled up. But the data proves otherwise—they are in layers, intact as species, none of them caught between their own kind (Gen. 1:11-12, 21-25; 6:20; 7:14). That's because that's how our Creator designed their DNA. The most fervent of wishful thinking and adding untold billion and billions of years (like McDonald's burgers) can't change God's design.

As Marine Biologist Robert Carter, PhD affirms: "People have heard the phrase 'the missing link,' and they usually think of between man and monkeys. But there are missing links from almost every major group of animals . . . and plants and bacteria throughout the entire fossil record."[53] The Creator's plan simply didn't allow

---

[52] David Satter, "100 Years of Communism and 100 Million Dead," *Wall Street Journal* (Nov. 6, 2017), https://www.hudson.org/national-security-defense/100-years-of-communism-and-100-million-dead.

[53] *Is Genesis History?* (1:04:34).

for it, and trying to push God out of His own creation worked only during our so-called Enlightenment years and Darwin's thinking when we didn't even know about things like germs, but biblical creationist scientists have caught up, and the world will never again be subject to such mass duping and God-eviscerating theories.

Imagine if humans had trusted God with their personal identity, instead of following their own deceitful, untrustworthy hearts (Jer. 17:9). Imagine how many young people could have been taught from birth that their infinite value, worth, and identity come from God, not their fleeting feelings. An editing client of mine recently did his doctoral project on this very subject after some young teenagers from his own family and his church began to struggle with identity, some wrestling with suicidal ideation. What pastor hasn't seen this, hasn't dealt with it, both at home and at church? It's not just one church's problem; it's a national, spiritual crisis.

Here is a quote from the above project by a man named Chris Morphew from England:

> If we're trying to figure out who we really are, we can't just go chasing after our deepest feelings and wants—because our feelings and wants change all the time, and they contradict each other, and they don't always lead us to healthy places. We can't just *be true to ourselves*. We need to choose which parts of ourselves to be true to. We can't just *follow our hearts*. We need to sort through what's *in* our hearts and figure out what to do with it all. And to do that, we need someone or something *outside* ourselves. We need some *other* voice that can help us sort through

all our thoughts and feelings and figure out who we really are, who we want to be, and how to actually live in a way that matches up with that.[54]

We understand what we see today through the ultimate lens and record of history in our oldest book, the Bible. By it, we understand where we came from, how the earth and everything around it came to be, and what it is the rocks today are crying out, and what it is the fossils are speaking out loud to ears that can hear and eyes that can see (Matt. 11:15). They are not like those who have the same ears and eyes but can't see or hear the truth. Why? Because they refuse to (Ezek. 12:2).

The Master Artist of Light and Truth and every conceivable stunning facet of creation and shade of humanity cannot and will not be silenced by the unbelievers among us, no matter how sincerely they cling to their idols or ideas crafted in spiritual darkness. One day, soon enough, they will all bow their knees, willingly or unwillingly (Phil. 2:10). Woe to them who call evil good and darkness light (Isa. 5:20)! I wouldn't want to be in their shoes when they are called to the throne!

There's light everywhere we look, even in the disasters of history and today's crises that seem ever present. God is the one constant who never changes. He's been busy for 2,000+ years creating a new heaven and new earth, without a Temple since God and the Lamb will be the Temple, where there won't be any need

---

[54] Chris Morphew, *Who Am I and Why Do I Matter?* (Epsom, England: The Good Book Company, 2022), 27-28. Italics original.

of light because the glory of God Himself will be the light, and the Lamb will be the lamp (Rev. 1:22-23).

The book began with a poem by Whit, and it's appropriate to end with one as well.

> you think
> you need fixing,
> but you only need space
> for light
> to move through you.
>
> the breaking was
> just another way
> to let light in.
>
> when your wounds
> become the windows,
> the light never leaves.[55]

Think about the wonder of God's amazing creation and sovereign activity among us. Scars become lights to illuminate the path for other scar bearers ... wounds become windows for others to see the light that shines within. As Whit puts it, "glow like you mean it." This is God's handiwork within and without, dispelling every shadow of darkness that invades humanity, driving out every sadness, and someday wiping away every tear ever shed, every memory of hurt, every iota of suffering, until

---

[55] Whit, *Revive Your Roar*, https://www.facebook.com/photo.php?fbid=746371158432604&set=pb. 100091791788573.-2207520000&type=3. While her writing isn't overtly Christian, per the discussion in Chapter 4, I have read more than 100 of her poems and her faith seems apparent to me.

only light and love will remain, as it was in the beginning, and then will be forevermore (Rev. 21:4).

In closing, the following is a memorable social media post: "The scars you share become lighthouses for other people who are headed to the same rocks you hit."[56] The last image is from a longtime friend in Florida, Felicia Velotta. She had a dream, wrote these words afterward, and had AI create an image to match what she saw in the dream. That her dream, poem, and art came along as the book was in its final stages was both timely and prophetic, poignantly capturing the book's essence!

When God cracks open what's been hidden, light pours out in ways you never imagined.

"And Jesus is the radiance of God's glory" (Heb. 1:3)

56 "Keep Your Foot on the Gas," Nightly Live Podcast, https://www.facebook.com/KeepYourFootOnTheGasLivePodcast/photos.

Bibliography

"Ark of the Covenant." www.Biblelieux.com

Beck, Richard. *Stranger God: Meeting Jesus in Disguise.* Minneapolis: Fortress Press, 2017.

Becker, Lyndsey. "Lighthouses." Ancient Engineering Marvels" (Oct. 18, 2024). https://ancientengineeringmarvels.com/lighthouses-ancient-engineering-marvels/.

Bible Repository. "Tongues of Fire." https://biblerepository.com/bible-verses-about-tongues-of-fire/.

Brueggemann, Walter. *The Message of the Psalms.* Minneapolis: Augsburg, 1984.

Christian Pure Staff. "Bible Study: Oil in Scripture and its Hidden Layers of Meaning." https://christianpure.com/learn/oil-in-scripture-meaning/.

Christ's Hope and Reconciliation Ministry (C.H.A.R.M.). https://charmprisonministry.org.

Creech, R. Robert. *Family Systems in Congregation Life.* Grand Rapids: Baker Academic, 2019.

Gibson, Mel, and Diane Sawyer. "Mel Gibson's *Passion*: Primetime Live Interview with Diane Sawyer" (2004): https://www.youtube.com/watch?v=7Ecnfe530IE.

Got Questions. "Shekinah Glory."
https://www.gotquestions.org/shekinah-glory.html.

Grant, Amy. "Lay Down" (the Burden of Your Heart). My
Father's Eyes (1979), https://genius.com/Amy-grant-
lay-down-the-burden-of-your-heart-lyrics.

Holy Land Site. "Wilderness Tabernacle."
www.holylandsite.com.

Hrebik, Kevin. "When Jesus Meets Your Scars." YouTube
(2025). 12 Lessons and 2 Interviews.
https://www.youtube.com/results?search_query=when
+jesus+meets+your+scars.

———. *Applying Faith and Family Systems to Emotional Scars.*
Amazon: KDP, 2024 update (original 2022).

———. *The Special Message of Jesus' Scars.* Amazon: KDP,
2023.

———. *Repurposing Scars: Meaningful Life after the Enduring
Damage of Trauma.* Amazon: KDP, 2022.

———. *The Carpenter's Shop and Other Metaphors.* Amazon:
KDP, 2022.

Keaggy, Phil. "Your Love Broke Through." Album and Song.
New Song Records, 1979.

"Keep Your Foot on the Gas." Nightly Live Podcast.
https://www.facebook.com/KeepYourFootOnTheGasL
ivePodcast/photos.

Kelley, Melissa. *Grief: Contemporary Theory and the Practice of
Ministry.* Minneapolis: Fortress Press, 2010
.

Knowing Jesus. "Shekinah Glory." https://bible.knowing-jesus.com/topics/God~s-Shekinah-Glory.

Kubler-Ross, Elizabeth. In Clemmer, Jim. *The Leader's Digest: Timeless Principles for Team and Organization*. Kitchner, Ontario: Clemmer Group, 2003.

Lewis, C. S. *The Space Trilogy: Out of the Silent Planet, Perelandra, That Hideous Strength*. NY: Simon and Schuster, 2011.

———. *Letters to Malcolm: Chiefly on Prayer*. San Diego: Harvest, 1964.

———. *Is Theology Poetry?* London: Geoffrey Bless, 1962.

———. *Reflections on the Psalms*. Boston: Houghton Mifflin Harcourt, 1958.

Morphew, Chris. *Who Am I and Why Do I Matter?* Epsom, England: The Good Book Company, 2022.

Nouwen, Henri. *Turn My Mourning into Dancing: Finding Hope in Hard Times*. Nashville: Thomas Nelson, 2022.

———. *The Inner Voice of Love: A Journey through Anguish to Freedom*. New York: Doubleday, 1996.

———. *Reaching Out: The Three Movements of the Spiritual Life*. New York: Doubleday, 1975.

Osborne, Grant. *The Hermeneutical Spiral: A Comprehensive Introduction to Biblical Interpretation*. Downers Grove: IVP Academic, 2006.

Salcy, Daniel, Josh Duffy, and Kevin Hrebik. "A Prison Story." 1LoveHTX Podcast (Season 4, Episode 112). https://www.youtube.com/watch?v=t6TghB2f9gw.

Satter, David. "100 Years of Communism and 100 Million Dead." *Wall Street Journal* (Nov. 6, 2017). https://www.hudson.org/national-security-defense/100-years-of-communism-and-100-million-dead.

Schweitzer, Mary, Jennifer Whitmeyer, John Horner, and Jan Toporsky. "Soft Tissue Vessels and Cellular Preservation in Tyrannosaurus Rex." *Science* 307, no. 5717 (March 25, 2005): 1952–55, https://science.sciencemag.org/content/307/5717/1952.full.

Johnson, Abby, Chuck Konzleman, and Gary Solomon. *Unplanned.* Pure Flix Entertainment, 2019. https://www.imdb.com/title/tt9024106/plotsummary/?ref_=tt_ov_pl.

Ventura, Diana. *Our Fractured Wholeness: Making the Courageous Journey from Brokenness to Love.* Eugene, OR: Cascade Books, 2010.

Weller, Francis. *The Wild Edge of Sorrow: Rituals of Renewal and the Sacred Work of Grief.* Berkeley, CA: North Atlantic Books, 2015.

Whit. *Revive Your Roar.* https://reviveyourroar.com.

Young, William P. "The Shack Summary." Lit Charts. https://www.litcharts.com/lit/the-shack/summary.

About the Author

Kevin Hrebik grew up in an extremely violent home, where he and his two brothers at the time (two more came later) were daily and often cruelly punished for the most trivial things.[57] He and brother Karl became especially close during the extended trauma, and later shared similar struggles in life, including both getting divorced, hitting rock bottom in their own ways, and both having emotional and relational issues. They ended up in seminary later in life and full-time ministry at the same time. Karl also recently wrote his first book.[58]

---

[57] See Kevin's full testimony with photos in *Repurposing Scars*, Appendix A. See detail in the Bibliography.

[58] Karl Hrebik, *Like a Tree: A Study Guide and Commentary from a Pastor's Heart*, Book 1: Psalms 1–41 (Amazon, KDP: 2025).

Kevin reacted quite badly after their dad's death in 1970. Upon leaving home at age 18, he promptly dove headfirst into the world of drinking and drugs, which scenario quickly began to take a major toll, and he became addicted to both. His failing mental and physical health from both the abuse and self-inflicted trauma created the perfect storm for God to intervene.

Upon becoming a Christian, his healing and transformation began in earnest, and while he had a long road ahead of him, God steered him toward a trajectory that would lead to many successes later in life: advanced education, acquiring four degrees, culminating in a Doctor of Ministry, extensive freelancing, professional editing, authoring several books, and also to many years of part time and then fulltime ministry. His own layered scarring, unjustly from his father and then by his own hand, and his protracted, hard-won recovery continue to inspire his teaching, writing, and ministry to the present.

Now retired, Kevin was a staff Chaplain for the Texas Department of Criminal Justice for ten years, serving at the largest female prison in the state, which houses up to 2,250 women. He served as a resident Chaplain for two years in the world-renowned Texas Medical Center, where he earned nine units of Clinical Pastoral Education. He was a volunteer Chaplain for several years at Harris County Jail in Houston, where he did human research for his doctoral project. He resides in Houston with his wife, Cara, who holds an MBA in global management and has enjoyed a full career of various financial/accounting jobs. As the time of writing, they celebrated 34 years of marriage. The photo is from

November 2024 when they were distributing Christmas cards to the inmates on the unit where he worked.

In retirement, Kevin continues to edit doctoral papers and dissertations, and directly related, he has been teaching "Doctoral Level Writing" on Zoom since 2012 to new seminary cohorts at Houston Graduate School of Theology (now with Kairos University), and in recent years to doctoral students from Baylor University's Truett Theological Seminary.

He has posted videos online of the family systems curriculum[59] that he taught for 13 years to thousands of both male and female inmates. The material is available on the Pando App (for inmates) and YouTube (for their families) through the podcasts of Less than the Least Ministries,[60] where he serves on their board of directors. He also speaks at various events about his curriculum, such as the annual Chaplaincy Leadership Forum in March 2024, where he was invited to speak for 2 hours to an audience of all the Texas unit chaplains and leadership in TDCJ. In September 2025, he was given a 3-hour slot to speak to jail, prison, regional, and federal chaplains at the Texas Baptist Correctional Chaplains annual conference.

The book you are holding continues the theme of Kevin's life work in the arena of emotional scars. As he mentioned earlier, "We may retire from a career, but we don't retire from our calling."

---

[59] Kevin Hrebik, *Applying Faith and Family Systems to Emotional Scars* (Amazon: KDP, 2022).

[60] Search on YouTube for "When Jesus Meets Your Scars." See the Preface for the URL in a footnote, p.xiii.

"And so, we have the prophetic word made more sure, to which you do well to pay attention as to a lamp shining in a dark place, until the day dawns and the morning star arises in your hearts" (2 Pet. 1:19).